Protecting Her Peace

GW00585062

Brooke Heberling

NEWMAN SPRINGS PUBLISHING
320 Broad Street
Red Bank, NJ 07701

First originally published by Newman Springs Publishing 2022

ISBN 979-8-88763-134-9 (Paperback)
ISBN 979-8-88763-135-6 (Digital)

Printed in the United States of America

For Derrick, Graham, and Anna Blue

CONTENTS

FOREWORD

You're Not Alone

Dearest Reader,

If you have found yourself opening the pages of this book, know that there is some part of you that is ready to heal. Trust that part no matter how many times your ego reminds you that you have tried and failed. It is the lifeline for a journey of healing and recovery from an eating disorder, addiction, trauma—whatever you carry inside of you that needs transformation.

I am so excited for you to get to know Ruby, the main character of this book. She found a way—repeatedly—to trust the part of her that wanted to heal. That part of Ruby is seen in how she wanted to love and be loved even when love hurt her. You see that part of her as a mother who was determined to break the chain of generational pain and dysfunction that she was born into.

And she did! This journey of change is real and possible for each of you. As you will learn from Ruby, there is no perfect, step-ordered, right, or wrong way of doing it. Like Ruby, we all do what works for us. Also, like Ruby, we just need to stay the course long enough to gather the experiences that lead to help and healing.

There are a few things I want to highlight about Ruby for you to notice as you get to know her in the pages of this book. She is easy to fall in love with, but these parts of her spirit were essential fuel for her journey of healing. They will help you, too, if you find a way to notice how you express them or embody them in your own life.

First is the wide-open way she authentically embraces all of her mess—her ugly, exquisite, dangerously daring mess! Ruby's willingness to get to know her mess, to allow it to emerge and to share it with others who were able to help her heal is inspirational. And we all can do this. It simply requires that we be real—first with ourselves, a little at a time, and then with another, also a little at a time.

The second essential aspect Ruby embodies is courage. Initially, she had dysfunctional courage fired by her pain and folded into her personality as her illness. As a reader, notice how you do *not* find yourself judging that kind of courage in Ruby. So be careful not to judge the level of bold dysfunction you find in your *own* life. Thank it! It is a part of you that is trying desperately to protect you from pain. Your dysfunction's intentions are good. It is just not adequately equipped to help you. Love the courage and tenacity of your illness. It will lead you to what needs healing inside of you.

Finally, Ruby embodies faith and a willingness to trust and ask for help. That faith also allows her to take the risk to love again, even when it hurts. Finding that place inside of you that has a sliver of willingness to ask for help and try to love again has huge payoffs. That part can be tiny and fleeting. It doesn't matter. It's like the mustard seed. The possibility of what it can become is miraculous! Ruby unabashedly allows that part of her to trust in love. She pursues help and sometimes just receives it even when her illness is scared to accept it. You can too.

There are so many things I love about Ruby. I know you will love her too. As you read and delight in her, be sure to see in yourself what you admire and appreciate about her. Learn to allow and align with those aspects of Ruby that are also in you. It is the fuel for *your* journey of healing. May you see the beauty inside of you and in the mirror, just like Ruby did!

With great love and admiration for the healing journey in these pages and for the one you are about to embark on in your own life.

Compassionately,
Leslie Fye
Licensed professional counselor and wounded healer

CHAPTER 1

Tuesday, February 23, 2016

I'm staring at the familiar computer screen, and the plastic chair is digging into my fragile pelvis, so I shift to try to relieve the discomfort. I keep staring at this damn assessment survey I have to fill out again before the real torture begins, and the results haven't changed since I was last here in January. I'm guilty of everything each question asks—every one.

1. Name: *Ruby Leigh Blue*
2. Age: *31*
3. Do you attempt to restrict calories? *Duh.*
4. Do you make yourself sick because you feel uncomfortably full? *Yes—or really if I eat anything.*
5. Do you struggle with thoughts of killing yourself? *Does "everyone would be better off without me" count?*
6. Do you struggle with self-harm behaviors? *Is running until I pass out self-harm?*
7. Do you consume alcohol? *Red wine is my only joy in life. Back off.*

8. Have you experienced trauma in the past that made you think negatively about your body? *insert "here's how you can eat and still be skinny" lesson here*

9. Do you have any medical complications medically because of your eating disorder? *Last night I did jumping jacks to jumpstart my dying heart...apparently it's now being classified as Bradycardia, not just my "runner's heart".*

10. Are you having trouble functioning in your everyday life? *Only when I got caught and had to stop...*

I'm a failure.

"Mrs. Blue, if you press submit—that big red button right there," the assistant Candy leaned over my shoulder and pointed her long finger at the screen as if I were incompetent, and I thought, *I may get into my first fist fight right here in the claustrophobic cubicle they call admittance.* "I'll take you back to see Dr. Sapphire now." She smiled way too big for her gig. It's just as bad as when the dentist smiles and says *oops* after they drill into an exposed nerve; it's not a good look. I follow her to the open door at the end of the hallway, and I see the doctor waiting for me. Her dog Sassy is in her normal spot on her lap, and she does not get up to greet me. Fine with me, I cannot stand being touched right now, not with me being *this* thin.

"Well, well, Mrs. Ruby Blue, I'm glad you finally called. I have been expecting to hear from you since the race was over a month ago."

I knew she'd rub this in. I've been seeing Dr. Sapphire weekly since the fall of 2015 when Michael said, "You will go to counseling, or the kids and I will leave you here to live alone with your eating disorder." She is one of the most

2

respected eating disorder specialists in the state of Georgia, but that doesn't mean she has to be such a *bitch*.

Bitch or not, she's *right*. I have been avoiding therapy after my last visit with her. It's the first time someone bluntly told me that I was selfishly choosing imminent death over the chance at life, and it scared the hell out of me.

Choosing death…

It was last October when shit really hit the fan. I had already run three marathons in 2015, and I spontaneously signed up for a relay race that ran from Chattanooga to Nashville. I thought I might lose Michael that night because he had discovered the credit card charge for the race fee, and he exploded in anger.

"Dammit, Rubes, I thought we talked about you slowing down on this marathon shit, and now this? A two-hundred-mile race? I mean, you can't be serious, right? This is a joke." He threw his phone on the couch and paced the carpet as he rubbed his hands through his hair that was begging to be cut.

"No, Michael, it's not a whole two hundred miles that I will run. I only will run forty-one miles of it." I lift my brows to force a smile, but even I can't stand my own pathetic desperation.

"Oh, only forty-one miles. My bad, Rubes." He dropped to his knees and buried his face in my lap on the couch. I awkwardly lifted my hands to rest on his back, but my eyes were unable to focus on anything but the space between the matter and the air. His arms wrapped around my waist and rubbed his hands up and down my back, hitting every rib at a deliberately sad pace. I felt his body buckle, and he sucked the air into his lungs and held it there for a good twenty seconds, and then he finally spoke after he let out the breath. "It's us or this eating disorder, Ruby," and I knew he meant it.

He got up, stood in front of me with a sadness that still haunts me to this day, and he went to our room and shut the door. I remember feeling a clenching pain in my chest. I put my face in my hands and folded what was left of me onto my lap. Panda rubbed his big face on my hanging elbow, and I released one hand to the ground to find his head to scratch. I love this big boy, but it's times like these that I miss the familiar feel of Mickey's presence. I lost a piece of my soul when he passed in my arms last fall; there's something special about the first living thing you are responsible for beside yourself that saturates you like a scar. My stomach growls and the vibration puts me in perspective. Nali will need to be fed bright and early. Hudson's morning routine is crucial for a day's success, and I'm gonna need to extend my runs to prepare for the race.

Run...

The race was a success from an Instagram post perspective, but the implosion that came behind the scenes was the real tea. Yes, I made it without dying, but one of Dr. Sapphire's predictions had come true. As I crossed the finish line with my tears of pain and agony from the miles streaking my face, I felt my heart drop to my stomach as soon as I locked eyes with Michael. He was standing in the left corner about twenty feet behind the rest of the crowd that had gathered to see the first place female ultrateam finish. His arms were hanging limply at his side, his stare was blank, and his posture, cold. There was no celebration in his eyes. He later told me that he envisioned the photo finish being a part of my funeral slideshow because I was dying right in front of him. Cheers erupted as the rest of my running-obsessed posse proudly joined me for the photo. There were hugs, laughter, and tears. Turns out, our anchor leg Emily blew out her knee on her last run, and Charleigh was sick as a dog from all the supplements, but not one of the team was willing to pass up the press. Pizza and beer were passed around the entire team, but I left my slice in the box. I took one sip of the beer, and tossed it in the trash.

I didn't actually eat anything until the next day. I wanted to feel the emptiness eat me alive.

The wolves were pacing.

Try as I could to be excited about the major running accomplishment I'd just achieved, Michael's face told the real truth. What I'd just done was *stupid*. I could feel my weak heart flutter in my chest; it's an involuntary action that once represented hopeful anticipation but now are terrifying screams of desperation and agony. I ran the race knowing that my heart may not fully recover from it, and on top of that, I had just put a nail in the coffin of my marriage.

Might as well just ruin everything at once, I suppose.

Dr. Sapphire's voice snapped me back to the present. "Well, I'm glad you didn't die!" She never sugarcoats anything, and I avoid her glare by staring at my nails that are bloody and picked down to the quick. "But I do have to point out, you lied to me about your weight. I thought you said that you were doing okay with the meal plan? That's how you convinced us all not to have you committed for even attempting the race. You ate! That's what we agreed on: that you would eat, Ruby."

I shifted in the seat, itching to get up and walk out.

"It looks like you have drastically dropped weight just in the last month. How often are you still using behaviors?" Sassy yips at me as if to back her mama up.

This question…it's always the worst.

Am I using behaviors? Of course I'm using behaviors. Look at me! I wake up at 4:00 a.m. and run until I pass out and then do it all again after a full day's work and parenting my own two children. I refuse to eat anything but homemade protein balls because I know the exact ingredients, measure them to exact perfection, and only portion myself out the minimal amount of calories needed to fake my brain into being grateful for the little nourishment I'm willing to expend. And if I go one smidgen beyond my allotted portion, I puke and curse myself for being so fucking weak as to need food to survive. Run, starve, eat, puke, repeat. I should make T-shirts.

Have they ever stopped? The behaviors don't stop; they shift. My eating disorder is a master of deception. Like a rebellious kid stealing liquor from his parent's stash, he will only pour from one bottle until it's almost noticeable, and then he will move to the next bottle to stay below the parent's suspicions. But at some point, the declining liquor will be noticed, and the kid's shift in demeanor will suddenly be explained. My eating disorder is that rebellious kid, and the harmful actions are the bottles. For years, I only used a little here and a little there to stay clear of discovery, but I've gotten stingy, and the empty bottles are just whistleblowing traders. I'll die on that mountain.

Have they only escalated since the last time I was here? I feel like my eating disorder can be compared to the progression of the telephone: although its discovery took years and years, its acceleration, once introduced, has been beyond compare. And in the past fifteen years, much like the phone, my disorder has become a monster that is out of control and unable to be stopped. When it began, my ED was a Nokia switch plate brick that had limited minutes. Now it's the latest iPhone with unlimited storage, and I don't even know how to control it.

I tried to tell her what I wanted to be true, and she wanted to hear, "I'm sticking to Dr. Parson's dietary plan, so I'm not sure what is going on." She's not fooled one bit.

"That's bullshit, Ruby, and you know it." Dr. Sapph is a Christian counselor that cusses like a sailor, and I respect the shit out of that. I'm not sure how one could navigate defeating eating disorders without swearing. "Is one behavior dominating over the others?" She is referring to my whack-a-mole nature with my three favorite Rs: running, restricting, and retching.

Simple answer: no. All the R's are raging at the moment. The answer you give to your therapist who is trying to convince you to check yourself into an impatient treatment center: watch and learn:

"I'm managing them well."

Well, maybe I was a tad overconfident in my anticipation of that profound answer.

Managing them well?

Like I'm a damn coach divvying out drills?

Idiot.

"We can sit here all night and play games, Ruby Blue, but you and I both know that is not going to get you any closer to freedom from this monster." She waits for my response, and I don't give her the satisfaction. She pulls out the printout of the survey I completed in the claustrophobic closet and shakes her head, parts her lips to show her perfect tooth gap, and laughs out loud. It seems like an odd response, but that's Dr. Sapphire. "I have your vitals, weight, and survey answers here, and I swear, Ruby, I'm afraid to let you out of this office. You're not stable. Your heart is failing. Your organs will not take much more deprivation. You need to go to Manna House. It's time." She looked me dead in my soul, and I stared back, unwilling to break. This has been her suggestion for over three months now, and there's an open bed lined up for a forty-fricking-five-day minimum stay at her treatment facility.

When I told my mom about the *opportunity* of inpatient care months ago, her response was, "What do they do, sit around and force feed you to fatten you up? Seems ridiculous to me." Ever since she spoke those words, all I can picture in my brain is troughs of food, napkins tucked into shirts, shovel-size spoons for efficiency, and knit-browed nurses with arms crossed waiting to pounce at any slight refusal from a patient. My mother's words have a way of sticking with me.

Don't cry, don't cry.

I swallow the tears that are rushing my lids with a vengeance. I think about Nali. Her blue-green eyes, sweet dimples, and her inquisitive round face. I can't just *leave* her. I'm her *mama*. She's only two years old. What if she needs me? What if she forgets me?

What if she's better off without me?

I shift my thoughts to Hudson. He's already showing so many anxious behaviors surrounding food, and he's only four.

Apple doesn't fall far...

He only eats sausage, broccoli, bread, and milk. Anytime I try to get him to try something new. he has an utter meltdown, and I can't handle forcing him to eat, so I give in to his food fears and limiting preferences. Michael doesn't have the patience for his meltdowns. He needs his mama!

And my students need me.

My family needs me.

My work needs me.

My cats need me.

There is no way...

There is just no way I can get up and leave my life for a *minimum* of *forty-five days!* I've heard of women who stay at those facilities for months and months.

Not this woman.

No fucking way.

But there's no way I can keep living like this either.

"I can't, Sapph. I can't." A weep escaped my mouth, and I let the tears overflow onto my raw cheeks. I look at her sitting across from me, and I'm begging, pleading with my eyes for some form of comfort, but she puts it right back on me. "You *can't afford not to,* Ruby. You really *can't.*" She pauses. "You're dying."

"No, I'm not."

"Wake up, Ruby. Yes. You. Are." Her big brown eyes were locked with mine, and I couldn't look away. "Don't you want to enjoy your time with your kids instead of constantly thinking about what you are going to put in your mouth or how you are going to get rid of it?"

Impossible.

"Don't you want to be close with Michael again, stop the redundant arguing, and rekindle that electric love you guys share?"

I've lied to him and betrayed his trust too much.

"Don't you want to write? Teach? Love? Connect? *Live?*"

Not like this.

My chin is chattering so loudly that I physically grip my jaw to stop the involuntary action. I sat in silence, not knowing how to answer her questions. As much as she pissed me off, she was right. My eating disorder has ruled me since I was fifteen, and my anxieties ran the show long before then. The wolves have paced, the darkness has saturated my mind, and my ED's won over and over and over again. I pictured myself being old, wrinkled, skin and bones, barely shuffling down the sidewalks, still desperately trying to drown out the abusive voice that's been my only constant companion in life because I pushed every other meaningful relationship to the brink of destruction just to prove myself right that no one ever truly has loved me and I'm not worthy of love and happiness in any way, shape, or form.

Forget this.

"You know what? I shouldn't be sitting here. I shouldn't even be in this goddamn position. You know why? You want to know why?" I found my footing, and I stood tall in front of that couch. "I wouldn't even be sitting here today if *she'd* gotten help! If *she* didn't hate her body, if *she* didn't talk shit about food, and if *she* didn't run the fuck away from all *her* problems, *I* would be *fine! I* would have never learned to hate myself so deeply. It goes *so deep.*" My fists are clenched, and I feel my legs begin to quake. "Here I'm thirty-one, and *I'm killing myself* because *she* didn't get help."

I was frozen in that moment of confession, and then Dr. Sapphire spoke.

"Do you want Hudson or Nali to be sitting on my couch in thirty years saying the same thing about you?"

The air left the room, and my throat felt as though it was about to collapse into my spine.

Do you want Hudson or Nali to say the same thing about you?

"I don't *ever* want them to *feel* what I have *felt.* I don't want them to *hate* their body like I have *hated* mine. I don't want them to think that they are only as good as their *physical abilities* or their *physical appearance.* I want them to *enjoy* food, friends, adventures. I want them to feel *safe* and *loved* and like the most important thing that ever walked the face of the earth! I want them to *thrive*, not just survive. I want them to *live*, not just exist. Dr. Sapph, I want them to be *nothing* like me." It all came out of my mouth faster than I could think, and the instant confess-regret was strong.

"So you need to heal so you *will* want them to be like you." Her voice is soft like a blanket.

I played into that perfectly.

This is the call to adventure. My own hero's journey. This is the mission if I choose to accept it. And if I don't, I will be the biggest hypocrite on the planet. I *don't* want my kids to be sitting here when they are my age, wishing that I had healed *my shit* so I didn't pass it on to them.

I know what I have to do.

I sit down on the couch, place my hands on my lap, and take a breath. "When do I leave?" I choked out and swallowed the tears along with my pride.

"Now." Dr. Sapphire states, and a soft smile crosses her lips. "Michael is waiting for you in the car."

"Okay," I said in defeat.

Yes.

I think I want to live.

Maybe.

CHAPTER 2

Saturday, October 16, 2021

I bought a full-length mirror for the first time in my thirty-seven years of life this morning. I was only at the store to get some last-minute items for Nali's birthday party later in the afternoon, but as I was pursuing mindlessly through the home section, its regal presence and profound energy caught my attention. I normally breeze by any mirror to avoid the urge to scrutinize some human aspect of myself that only I would notice, but something within forced me to stop this time.

The mirror was about six feet tall, had an antique gold trim, and was freestanding like the ones I've seen in the staged homes I dream about while scrolling through Zillow. I've taken up the habit comparing my affordable suburban shoebox to the intricate custom-crafted cabins nestled in the woods near the streams.

A girl can dream.

I stood there in the middle of the aisle, staring at my reflection with a gentleness that I'd never experienced before. I reached up to smooth my light-brown hair. It's long, straight, and it frames my heart-shaped face that can be described as both wide and sharp at the same time. My broad shoulders are squared off as if I wear shoulder pads twenty-four seven, but they parallel pleasingly to my strong jawline. My sun-kissed skin made my blue eyes demand pause. I've always thought of myself as more handsome than beautiful, and for most of my life, I've resented inheriting the masculine features.

I was dressed casually, as normal, in ripped mom jeans and a long crop top that only exposed a sliver of my belly and my river shoes to remind me of where I belong. I get mistaken for a student in the halls of the high school where I teach almost daily, but when I turn around and they see my face, it's the crow's-feet that give away my true generation affiliation: "geriatric millennial." As if attending school in the 2000s with the low-rise trends, the pierced-belly button requirement, and Britney Spears's tramp stamp standard wasn't enough, we now own the title of "geriatric".

Can I sue MTV? Pretty sure TRL Spring Break had everything to do with ninety percent of insecurities back then.

I took a deep breath in, and my chest rose toward the fluorescent lights above. I felt the tingles of the pressure attempting to escape my lungs, and I audibly let the air release to give relief. My brain's still learning to recognize the new figure staring back at me, but I continue to toy with accepting my newfound fullness rather than beating myself up for not having abs and a sub-six-mile time.

I'm so damn tired of being scared of my changing physical presence in the world. It's sad that women have been given a shelf life by society that determines an expiration date for beauty and worth. If I drown out all the noise around me, I can actually hear my wise mind admitting, *You're quite beautiful, Ruby Blue.* It's weird too because not only am I starting to hear it, but I'm starting to see it too. If we're all made of the same material as the stars like famous author Don Miguel Ruiz says, then the beauty of humanity is nonnegotiable.

I'm no exception.

The loudspeaker blared a scratchy, "Good morning, fashionistas!" I was suddenly flushed, and I felt sweat pool in my Chacos. I shifted my eyes left and then right, and sure enough, a woman was staring at me as if I just licked the glass. I snatched up the mirror in the crook of my good arm and awkwardly trudged to the cashier adjusting my awkward grip the entire way.

After miraculously getting it home without breaking the oversized thing, I sat it up in the corner of my bedroom between the cat tower my dad and Hudson found on the side of the road and the dirty clothes basket that's in a constant state of overflow. I cock my head to the side, assess my design decision, and all I can think of is how out of place it looks.

Go figure.

I stared into the looking glass at the body that's taken me years to find peace with, and it wasn't until I was here in the comfort of my own bedroom that I began to regret the impulsive buy. Funny how that works. In the middle of the home section with complete strangers surrounding me, I was confident in my reflection. Now in the solitude of my own four bedroom walls, I'm doubting how I ever thought I deserved such an extravagant luxury. I threw the nearest blanket over the glass, and I exited the bedroom quickly.

*****

"Are you ready for the best birthday party ever, my girl?"

God bless my children. I've set their standards really low since day one with parties. I'm not a Pinterest mom at all. In fact we're lucky if I remember to even buy the cake, but I've really tried to make this one special for my girl.

I hope she feels it.

I grabbed Nali's hands and twirled her around in a circle and then placed my hands in her armpits and hoisted her up into my arms as we've done a million times before. She let out a squeal and dug her nose into my cheek. She may be turning eight, but she's still my baby.

"Yes, Mama! I'm *so* excited! When's everyone going to be here?" She throws her head back and lets her arms fall to the floor, trusting I'll counteract her gravity defiance with my strength, but she's not a baby anymore! Thank God I'm prepared, and I catch her right before she slips from my grasp.

"Nali! You are getting way too big to do that, Love! You're going to bust your head open! I would like to have your sleepover here, not at the children's hospital!" I shake my head as she smiles at me and cartwheels out of my arms to immediately run as if I'll chase her. Her dismount triggers a memory, but it's not clear.

Déjà vu is like that.

When I say that we are frequent flyers at the children's hospital in town, I mean Nali Blue should have a wing named after her! RSV as a three-week-old, a deadly reaction to penicillin, toxic synovitis (I had to look it up too), and two concussions in one day. Homegirl is a hot mess.

She get it from her mama.

"Hey, Mama!" Hudson yells for the eighteenth time in ten minutes. "When's Papa getting here to pick me up? I don't want to be here when all the *girls* come."

Oh, Hudson. He has my heart, but man did he get the brunt of my anxiety. He had colic when he was born, and his first four months of life almost killed me. He would cry from four o'clock in the afternoon to ten o'clock at night, and since Michael was in the middle of his first basketball season as a head coach, I was mostly faced with navigating the role as a new parent on my own. My dad was my savior those first few months Hud was born. He would come over daily to hold the disgruntled first grandbaby, and Papa knew he was the only person that could make it better. They've had a soul connection since day one, and I still feel my heart bursting when I see them together.

"Where's Daddy?" he asked next, and I repeated a phrase that's well known by all.

"He's at work, but he should be here any minute."

"But it's Saturday?"

"He's at a golf tournament."

"Lucky."

My thoughts exactly.

Michael's a workaholic, and he has an unhealthy want to be needed by those around him. Although I think that was his initial draw to me, but now it's definitely easier to check off work tasks that'll get him constant praise from his boss than to be home and face the discomfort and lack of connection with his exhausting wife and kids.

In fairness, I was a dumpster fire for a long time, but I needed to learn how to put the flames out, not be left alone to burn.

There's a big difference.

When we first met, he would stay at the gym so late that I used to think he had another girlfriend. To me, there was no way he could be "at work" so late. Even though he'd reassure me daily that he was just with the athletes, I was still secretly questioning his whereabouts and motivations for being gone *so* late *so* often. One night, I remember sneaking up to the New Hope basketball gym at 11:00 p.m., fully expecting to catch him in the act.

The gravel popped and cracked as I pulled slowly into the gym's side lot. If I was going to catch him, I knew I had to be sneaky about it. I rolled into the open spot next to his teal Dodge Dakota Sport, and I opened my door as quietly as possible.

Bang! Like a shot from a gun, a giant figure burst through the side door of the rusty building and scared the hell out of me. I let out a scream that I instantly wanted to swallow back down no matter how painful, but it was too late. I was caught, caught spying on my not-cheating boyfriend by a student.

Malcom, in his six-foot-ten glory, yelled out, "What's good, Ms. Brooks?" He had a clear garbage bag with cans slung over his shoulder to give his parents to recycle. Five cents a can adds up if you need the cash, and his family did.

"Mal, man, you scared me!"

"Sorry 'bout dat. Coach's kickin' us out."

"Were y'all practicing? At 11:00 p.m.?"

"Naw, Blue lets us chill here and ball so we don't have to go to the concrete cort in Columbus after dark. Booney got jumped last month, and Coach's tryin' keep us out the back seat of the 5-0 defending our boi, ya herd."

"Well, that's nice of him. Drive safe, bud."

"I walk, Ms. Brooks."

"Right. Walk safe."

"Yes, ma'am. Treat my main man Blue right! Sorry we keepin' him from ya."

I'm a literal piece of shit.

I said something to the effect of, "Don't worry how I treat my man. You better worry how you treat your grades," and he laughed and shook his head at my lame attempt to play off the stalking. It's a bizarre thing, teaching eighteen-year-olds when you're only twenty-two. Although *I* understood the vastness of that four-year age gap, the students didn't always see it that way, especially when *they* hooked me up with *their* college-aged coach. I'm pretty sure I stole him from a senior's sister in my creative writing class.

Michael must have heard Mal greet me because he strutted out of the slowly closing doors into the damp, sticky night.

"Hey, Rubes, what are you doing here?"

Caught.

It was then I realized that I'd shown up unannounced without a plan of what to do if he *wasn't* caught cheating.

"I thought you might be hungry because it's late, ya know."

Good recovery.

"Yeah, sorry. It's impossible to get these kids to leave. They'd play all night if I'd let them. I told them to be out by eleven thirty, so they should be gone soon, *right, guys?*" He directed that last word to the five sweaty ballers that looked as if they were in no hurry to leave. "It's nice of you to think of me! I'm actually really hungry. Whaddya bring?"

Shit.

The food offer was a decoy I hadn't thought through thoroughly, so I stood there in awkward silence as he leaned forward as if he could better hear my internal response if he listened close enough. I said the first thing that came to mind.

"Man, I just remembered I fed it to Mickey." *Lie.* "It was shrimp." *Also a lie.* "It's his favorite." *Truth! It actually is his favorite.* Michael's still warming up to Mickey. He didn't grow up with pets, much less cats.

"You're so crazy."

I giggle shyly, "You have no idea."

"Did you really come up here to bring me food?"

"Maybe…or maybe I was just missing you."

Flirtation has always been my superpower.

He walked closer to me. "Well, if Mickey finished up the shrimp, then why don't we swing by Little Dooey's on the way home to get the chicken you like? I'm in the mood for barbecue. They're open till the meat's gone tonight. Booney's mama is on the grill. She'll hook us up."

That was the first time I lied to Michael.

That night, we got fresh fried chicken from Booney's mama, and I threw it up minutes after I woofed it down along with a salad and a side of mac 'n' cheese in the porta-potty behind the restaurant.

I'm not proud.

As long as it took me to own up to my eating disorder, it's taken him *longer* to break his work habits. What was once a sweet gesture to keep high school boys off the streets soon became one more scouting video, one more run through of a drill, one more set of one hundred free throws to solidify the money shot. Back then, it was like he was working on helping them because I refused to allow him to help me. So I get how hard it was at the time, but I've been (mostly) clean of my disorder for five years now, so I can't be blamed for his lack of participation in this family anymore.

"Bud, he'll be here any minute. Patience, my dude. Patience."

Hudson ran out the front door, smacking the party balloons with a vigor that only a ten-year-old boy can, and Nali let out an annoyed grunt and proceeded to fix them to her specifications.

They drive me nuts, but I'm truly blessed to be their mama.

"Knock, knock!" Camryn opens the door, and her daughter Roe slips through the open crack and runs straight for Nali's arms. Nali hugs her tightly, and Roe lifts one foot in glee and giggles with a smile that could melt Mount Everest. Camryn's my best friend. We met six years ago at work, and we've been an unstoppable duo ever since. There's not many people on this earth that I can truly be myself with, but I never have to censor my words, feelings, or actions with Cam. She gets me.

Everyone deserves a friend like her.

Roe is her five-year-old daughter, and she's like my third child. They live across the street now that Camryn's divorced is final, and Michael and I are her only family, and I've made it my mission to show her what a family can really be. I love Cam. She helps me not feel so alone.

"Hey, guys! Roe, are you so excited for your first sleepover?" She screams, "*Yes!*" and disappears into Nali's bedroom to play.

"Need any help?" Camryn offers, and I hand her a platter.

"Can you ice these cupcakes? You know I suck at the aesthetics." I'm not afraid to admit my flaws. I now try to live by the quote, "If you own your shit, no one can hold it against you."

"Sure! Where's Michael?" she asks as she delicately picks up the first Funfetti cupcake to frost.

"He's at a golf tournament for work, but he should be here any minute." I need a button to push anytime someone asks me this question that will instantly repeat, "*he's at work,*" to save my breath. I put the finishing touches on the fruit tray that the girls will devour, and I head over to the sink to wash the veggies next.

I remember parties being so special as a kid. Pony rides in the front yard, Slip 'N Slides that end too soon and leave you with scrapes on your belly for days. I always loved my birthday. Now that I'm in charge of that joy for my own kiddos, I feel such a pressure to create the magic that my mom did for me, yet something always seems to go wrong.

"What's uppppp!" Michael comes barreling through the front door, and before he even takes two steps over the threshold, I can smell sun and beer seeping out through his sweat. He's not a frequent drinker, but like many things in his life, he has a hard time understanding his limits. Michael's been a one-to-ten type of person lately, and it looks like we are on level ten today.

I will be handling this party on my own once again.

"Geez, Michael, did you leave any beer for the rest of the golfers? You weren't driving, were you?" I roll my eyes and continue to rinse the carrots.

"Oh, babe, it was just a work thing. I'm here now! Dan drove me. No worries! How can I help?" He plops down on the couch, pulls out his phone, and immerses himself in the world of mindless scrolling.

"Don't worry. I've got it covered." Camryn and I lock eyes, and we both shake our heads at the same time.

Sometimes I feel like he takes advantage of my hands-on parenting style. My mom was so loving toward me when I was a child, but she was going through hell basically my whole adolescence, so I was mostly left to take care of myself. I swore when I became a mother, I would be present and there for my kids. Little did I know how hard that truly is to do. It's not Michael's lack of willingness to jump in to help because he always offers. It's that he mostly uses his offers as a formality to be able to say, "I asked you if I could help!" We have been through so much trauma due to my disorder in our fifteen years together, and I often let him off the hook for the little acts of laziness out of sheer guilt. My anxiety, my eating disorder, and my need for control often were the root causes of all our issues, so my doing what I can, when I can is almost my way of making it up to him. Is it a healthy way to handle parenting our kids? *No.* Does it keep everyone happy? *Yes.*

Everyone but me.

Once the food was all out, the crafts were set up, and the games were prepped and ready to go, I realized that I forgot the sodas in the back of my car.

"Michael, can you please go get the drinks? They're in my trunk," I asked, and he shot up like I just fired a gun.

"On it! Got it! Right away!" He sprinted to the door, and he turned and looked at Camryn. "Hey, Cam, come help me for a sec." And he left the door open so she could follow him to the driveway.

"He's such a mess, Ruby! Don't worry. I will go make sure he doesn't drop them all." She finished the last cupcake and whipped her hands on the kitchen towel. I mouthed, *Thank you,* and turned my attention to getting the piñata set up.

I feel so lucky to have Camryn for sanity and support. I've had a few great girlfriends in my seasons of life, but Cam's acceptance of all my flaws and all my quirks gives me a level of comfort that I have only ever felt with Michael. I remember the day we first met. She was assigned to be my coteacher six years ago in my ninth grade collaborative classroom, and the second she walked in, we knew we would get along. We were literally wearing the same color skinny jeans with a similar striped top, and when I saw that her background on her phone was her three-legged cat, I knew it was fate. In the days that followed, we discovered that our sick sense of humor and love for the outdoors matched just as perfectly as our style, and here we are!

She filed for divorce from her high school sweetheart two years ago, and after a long, drawn-out process, she is finally free of the judgment, pressure, and ridicule that came from marrying a preacher's son. I'm proud of her. She did the self-work that was necessary to heal, and she's battled her way to happiness. Now she's dating a cool musician who treats her as if she's hung the moon. She told me from the start that divorce didn't scare her, but being miserable with her ex-husband for the rest of her life did. She's seen her mother stay in a loveless marriage for the principle of keeping a vow, and I see why her experience would encourage her to seek something more. My experience with divorce did the opposite for me. My parents had love, but immaturity and pride didn't do them any favors. They divorced when I was seven years old.

If Michael ever leaves me, I'm going with him.

Camryn is also very beautiful. She has eyes that are the color of a rare turquoise sea, and her laugh is the kind that makes others wish they knew the joke. Her dark humor kills me, and I can always count on her to help me in a moment's notice. The other day, I barged in on her at-home dinner date with Adam because I needed moral support to switch out my nose ring. I know it sounds stupid, but it meant the world that she'd pause everything just to metaphorically hold my hand while I painfully twisted the metal through the raw and healing hole in my nose.

Solidarity.

Learned that at Manna.

A few weeks ago, Cam and I made our best friend status official by getting matching moon phase tattoos. I have three so far: one on my butt and two on my wrist. The one on my ass is embarrassing, but the wrist tattoos I have are priceless. One is a Bible verse: "*I am that I am*" (Exodus 3:14). It's a daily reminder that God's in control and to be careful not to attach negative thoughts and feelings with my body. The moon phases represent that change is inevitable, and that having a soul partner in this world makes the dark times bearable. I thought it'd always be Michael and I against the world, but Cam's feminine energy in my corner feels new and exciting.

The door opens, and Camryn walks through it holding the two-liter bottles of Sprite and Coke. She looks pale. I put down the piñata and slowly walked over to help her with the bottles.

"Are you okay?" I reached for the sodas without breaking her gaze.

"Yeah, I just remembered I have to let the dogs out." She struggled to get the words out, so I knew that wasn't it.

"You and Roe just left the house. They were just outside!? What's really wrong? Where did Michael go?" I set the sodas on the counter and turned back just in time to see her slipping out the front door.

"I'll be right back." She forced as she shut the door behind her, and I was left staring at the hauntingly empty room confused as to what just happened.

Before I had any time to investigate her mood change and Michael's disappearance, there was a knock at the door. I wipe the water from washing off my hands and reach for the knob. I take a deep breath and open the door.

Whatever this is, it has to wait.

It's Nali's day.

"Who's ready to party?" I declare as the door swings open, and Nali's best friend Adda is standing there with her suitcase dragging her right shoulder uncomfortably down. Her hands were full of kid-wrapped present. She dryly smiled and handed the wrapped gift over to me.

"This bag is way too heavy. I think my mom packed me for a month!" She breezes past me and heads straight for

24

Nali's room. I heard the door rattle its normal tune and then shut once more.

As the party guests trickle in, I try to text Michael: *Where are you? The girls are all here, Hudson is with Papa, and they are already begging to open gifts. I could use a little help!* No response.

*****

After about thirty minutes, Camryn comes back through the door, but she doesn't look any better than when she left. Her face is ghost white and her eyes are puffy.

"Ruby, I have to talk to you." She said it quietly enough that the girls making slime at the counter did not even notice, and all the others were content outside playing on the trampoline, so now was our best option.

"Sure, come back to my bedroom," I offered, and we walked in silence down the hall.

We have a small house by choice. I used to relieve my anxiety by starving, puking, or running, but ever since treatment, my preferred method of numbing out has been cleaning. It was getting so overwhelming for me to constantly be cleaning and picking up our huge house that we didn't use half of, so we sold our first home, used the money to pay off all my medical debt, and downsized to what I like to call my "Joanna Gaines trailer." It's not actually a mobile home, but it sure is shaped like one, and the size is ultramanageable for our bank account and my OCD but not our sanity. We are too crammed in here, and although I love living under our means, I'm ready for a house that has at least two doors of separation when I'm trying to have a conversation in private.

25

As I closed the bedroom door behind us, Camryn sat down on my neatly made bed. She finally looked up, and her eyes searched mine with pain.

This isn't good.

"Did someone die? Are you okay? What's going on?" I sat down next to her, and she put her head in her hands.

"Ruby, I don't know how to say this." She paused and turned to look me in the eyes. Tears were brimming her bottom lids, and I swallowed hard.

I can't breathe.

"When I went out to help Michael get the drinks...he *hit* on me." A tear fell from her ocean eyes, and my stomach jumped straight into my throat.

"*What?*"

"He hit on me, Ruby, like for real. We both know Michael can make jokes, but this was not like that. He was being one hundred percent serious. I know he's been drinking, but he really made me uncomfortable." She wiped the tear off her cheek, and all I could do was stare at her in disbelief.

"What the hell did he say?" My mouth was bone-dry, and my brain felt like a '90s Windows screen saver bouncing aimlessly off the corners of my skull.

"He asked me to *come help him satisfy you in the bedroom.* I told him to shut up, and I tried to laugh it off, but then he cornered me up against the back hatch of your car, and he said it again: "*Come help me satisfy Ruby in the bedroom. It could be just what we all need to spice things up!* and I immediately pushed him away from me." She sniffed, and I continued to stare in complete shock. "Ruby, I swear I don't know where any of this came from. I mean, I literally ran home and sat on my couch, crying for the past thirty minutes, trying to figure out what to do."

I feel the bile creeping up my throat.

"I didn't ask for this, Ruby. As soon as I told him, 'That will be a *hard no!*' he backed off and started walking down the street."

I swallow for the first time in what seems like forever. My teeth violently slam together as if I just jumped in a river in January.

A threesome?

Is he insane?

I mean, am I not enough?

Does he just want Camryn and doesn't have the balls to say it to my face?

What a coward.

Thank God she said no!

What if she'd said yes?

"What are you doing?" Cam's pleading look breaks my heart. I begin to feel the anger overriding the shock, and it's as if I'm having an out-of-body experience.

"I'm texting Michael. I don't care if he drank the golf course out of commission, this is beyond messed up. How could he do this to you? How could he do this to me? Us?" The words tasted like sour milk as I spit them into existence. My fingers are shaking as I type a phrase I've only seen play-out on a movie screen, *"I know what you said to Cam. Don't come home tonight."*

This is my nightmare.

Nali burst through the door, and both Camryn and I desperately wipe our faces to get rid of the evidence.

"Mama, we are ready to do the piñata! Come on!" and before she can even register the mood in the room, she disappears into the hallway full of giggles and squeals. I turn my attention back to Cam.

"I don't even know what to say. I'm so sorry that he did that to you! What the hell was he thinking? I mean, *really?*" My anger's boiling over, and I grip my hands so tightly that they begin to go numb. My best friend—he hit on my best friend.

"Like, not to be weird, but have you guys ever talked about a threesome in your marriage?" I flush with heat.

How could he put me in this position?

I want to run.

I want to run until I collapse.

"Not even close! We don't even watch porn! This is literally out of nowhere...and that he involved you." I lace my fingers together and challenge each hand to win the tug of war as I place my white knuckles against my taut lips.

Is this my fault?

"I don't know what to do." My voice cracks, and Camryn places her arm around my shoulder and pulls me close.

He knows I can't handle this.

A sickening feeling hits me all at once.

How will we recover from this?

"I feel so bad. I've been sitting at my house, trying to think if I did anything to make him feel like that was an appropriate question to ask me, but I truly can't see it, Ruby. I really can't. For once, I can proudly say that I didn't ask for this." She holds her shoulders high, and as broken as I feel, I'm proud of her at this moment.

But being proud of her means my husband is the asshole.

He's a lot of things, but he's never been the asshole.

"You've done nothing wrong. This is just insane. I mean, really out of nowhere. It makes me question everything, you know?" I choke back tears, and Cam pulls me closer.

After everything we've been through, this is what's going to break us? I know I've been in love before but nothing like the love I share with Michael. No, he was not my first love. That was Marco. No, he was not my perfect fit. That was Weston. Michael was, is, and always will be my person, but he may have just fucked it all up.

I thought I was enough for him.

"I know. I hate that he did this to you, to me, to our *kids.*" That's when her voice cracks.

The kids...

I throw my hands up and let them slap my thighs with force on the way down. "Well, what do I do now? I can't call off the party, it will kill Nali!" I suck in a sob, and Cam nods. And then, like mother's often have to do, we make the silent agreement to shove the pain down below the surface, and it becomes the proverbial beach ball that threatens to explode through the placid surface at any moment with one false move.

I thought I got rid of the beach balls in my life.

As we walk into the chaos of the eight-year-old fun, I put on the front that I've learned to do since my childhood. I hear my parent's voices creep back in:

"You're fine, Ruby."

"You're overreacting, Ruby."

"You're lucky, Ruby."

"Just be grateful, Ruby."

If I'm okay, then why the hell do I feel like I'm about to crawl out of my skin? I look at my phone to see if Michael has responded. He did. It said only this:

"I fucked up. I'm sorry."

I slam the phone face down on the granite and swallow my whimper before it escapes my lips.

He didn't deny it.

Is this the beginning of the end?

The front door creaks, and I hear a low and long snuff of air as if a hungry animal is sniffing the cupcakes through

29

the small crack that lets a sliver of light from the porch. I hear a faint scratching, and I whisper to myself and myself alone, "Fact-check, Ruby. Fact-check. There are no wolves."

Then I hear the faint, *scratch, scratch, scratch.*

*****

My window is open so I can feel the cool night air hit my face. Now that all the girls are passed out in droves on the living room floor, I can let the tears freely pool in my pillow. My chest is sore from heaving, and the skin below my eyes is so raw that I'm afraid I may have actual scabs when I wake up. I've been dividing up assets and creating the perfect North Carolina job opportunities in my mind, and I jump out of bed before my spiraling thoughts take me to another level of consciousness that is not so easily controlled.

Nothing feels safe.

I tiptoe through the snoozing sleeping bags, and I reach for the lock of the front door. I told myself I wouldn't look out the window and give him the satisfaction of knowing I cared, but I couldn't resist the temptation. There in the driveway is Michael's truck. He is sitting on the back of the tailgate, and for a split second, I think about going out to talk to him, but as I put my hand on the knob, I hear a whisper.

"Mrs. Ruby? Are you leaving us?" Adda's anxious voice is quivering, and it almost breaks my heart for the seventeenth time today.

"Oh no, honey, I'm just locking up! I'm right here for the night! No worries. Do you need anything?"

"No, thank you." In one graceful flop, she rolls over in the pile of stuffed animals the girls collected and buries her face into the hippo Michael won at the fair after spending over one hundred dollars at an "impossible shot" game that *had* to be rigged. Michael just kept pointing, shooting, and hitting the target dead on, and *still*, nothing happened! The guy running the thing just gave it to him after a while because he felt sorry for him. I thought it was hilarious, but Michael was big mad. The hippo still makes me smile.

Well, it used to make me smile.

A flush of nausea comes over me, and I quickly run to the bathroom and lift the lid just in time. I'm always letting him off the hook for things, not holding him accountable for his actions—or lack thereof—because of the guilt I feel from *my* breakdown years ago.

But not anymore.

I'm *done.*

I go back to our bedroom, and a hopeful Murphie follows me. She is my orange cat that is a lush for attention and often at the most inopportune moments. Tonight, I'm thankful for her company. Her wet nose aggressively nudges my elbow to move, and she slips in the space between my torso and my left arm. I adjust to let her get comfortable, and I think of Michael outside in the bed of his trunk. I'm relieved he is home safe but mad at myself for caring.

Why did he have to be so stupid?

*****

Sleep definitely was a sidenote to spiraling thoughts, made-up scenarios, and a personal production of fake conversations in my head that will probably never come to fruition. I thought about my parents, their whirlwind relationship and rushed marriage that ended abruptly, and although it's my biggest fear, Michael and I tragically seem to be heading down the same road. I let my brain go to the place of *"this is exactly how their relationship began to break down,"* and the thought makes me sick to my stomach. It's not the comment Michael made. The comment is the blood on the carpet, not the reason for the murder. The wolves have returned to the scene of the crime, and they're ready to feast.

I remember being that scared little girl who couldn't fathom why her parents didn't want to be together anymore, and I swallow hard.

We can't do this to our kids.

We just can't.

*****

In the morning, his truck is gone, but there are two dozen doughnuts left on the front step for the girls when they wake up. It's our birthday tradition to have fresh doughnuts for breakfast, and the gesture makes me both smile and cringe. I smile because the small action shows he cares. I cringe because if he hadn't messed up, he'd be here eating them with us. Is this our life now? Is this how it will be?

"Dada dropped off doughnuts, Mama! The *good* kind!" Nali's face is covered in glaze flakes from the chocolate twisty she's devouring, and I force a grin.

"Yes, that was so nice of him!" The fake enthusiasm tastes sour.

"Where is he? It's Sunday morning? Does he have work today?" she questioned.

"I guess so, baby. Can I have a doughnut?" She hands me my favorite apple fritter, and I attempt to take a bite. It feels like a brick sliding down my throat, and I put the remaining pastry on the napkin in front of me.

What the hell am I going to do next?

"Thanks for such a great party, Mama! It was the best!" Nali wraps her arms around me and hugs me with closed eyes and a doughnut-filled grin.

"Anything for you, Nali Blue."

What am I gonna do next?

I heard a faint howl in the distance.

CHAPTER 3

Friday, August 30, 1991

My bedroom's dark—too dark. I pile my green blankie over my face in an attempt to hide from the wolves that I know pace through my room at night, but it's pointless.

They know where I sleep.

Mom and Dad say it's just my imagination, but I know they're real. *I feel them.* I wish Charleigh would let me sleep with her. The wolves don't come around when I'm with her. Maybe it's because she's older, or maybe she's just braver than me, and they know that? She's strong. I wish I was strong like her.

I can't sleep.

I can never sleep.

Lightning illuminates the room completely, and I press the blankie firm over my eyelids so hard that the blackness transforms into a swirl of purple and red, and I watch the colors dance in front of my brain. It reminds me of the kaleidoscope I always look through in the mall. Lightning cracks again, and my color show ends abruptly. My eyes shoot open, and my heart begins to pound in my chest like a drum. I don't hear any rain. Weird. Maybe it's heat lightning? Whatever that means.

I want Mom and Dad.

I slide off the side of my bed. The floor feels unsafe as I allow my nightgown to slowly fall down below my knees. It's August in Georgia, so it's hot, but I always feel more secure with layers of blankets and clothing. I think maybe the wolves won't be able to smell that I'm a little girl.

I stay on my tippy-toes to minimize the creaks that riddle the floor as I creep into the hallway. Mom doesn't let me sleep in the bed with them, but if I'm really quiet, I can crawl past her side of the bed and slip under the covers with Dad. He doesn't even wake up, and I can usually make it to morning snuggled up next to him. He snores pretty loudly, but it's worth it to feel safe. The wolves don't mess with me when I'm near my dad.

Once I'm in the foyer, I'm fully exposed by the light of the moon coming through the huge window over the front door. I see the trees bending in the wind when another flash stops me in my tracks. I plug my ears and brace myself for the loud crack. I close my eyes and count…

One Mississippi, two Mississippi, three Mississ—

Boom ba boommmmm ba boommmmm! I feel each extended roar of the sky rumble in my chest, and I crouch down by the railing of the stairwell that sits adjacent to the front door. I grasp the broken column, and I cringe. I fell off the balcony a few weeks ago. Charleigh and I made up a game called "human baseball" in the upstairs hallway, and that night, I took it too far, as they say I always do.

Man… Charleigh would actually play that game with me too.

I ruined it.

I ruin everything.

We have a souvenir blow up bat that we bought at Atlanta-Fulton County Stadium at the Atlanta Braves game we went to back in June, and the game goes like this: one of us is the batter, and one of us is the ball. The batter takes her stance at the end of the hall by the bonus room, while the person who is the ball bends over at the waist and wraps her arms around the back of her legs in a forward fold. The batter swings, hits the *ball* on the butt as hard as she can, and depending on how hard the hit is, the person who is the ball will forward roll down the hall in accordance to the power behind the swing. It's really fun! I like to stand like Ron Gant.

He sticks his butt out really far.

It was a particularly loud night in our house because Dad's boss was in town to travel with him, and they were drinking beers at the kitchen table one floor below us. It was my turn to be the ball, and Charleigh was the batter. We had been playing for about twenty minutes, and I knew that my big sister's willingness to interact with me was almost shot, so I had a plan to extend the fun.

It seemed like a good idea at the time.

I took my forward bend position and sang out, "Play ball!" Charleigh kicked her knee up so high, it hit her chest, and when she whipped her arms around, I felt the swoosh of the wind, and the inflatable bat hit me square on the tush.

She's surprisingly strong.

I executed the plan to make this an epic home run to keep her interested, so I began to forward roll with a ferocity that'll surely stroke her ego. Now that she's eight, she tries to act like she doesn't like playing "kid stuff," but somehow, she's right in the mix barking rules and bossing me around. I know she secretly loves me "making her play those dumb games."

Why do people want to be grown so badly?

It seems stressful.

"Home runnnnn!" I declared as I was flipping and flipping, and that's when it happened. I grossly misjudged the hallway length and barreled right into the wooden posts of the railing at top speed. Charleigh screamed, but the snap of the railing was ringing in my ears. I felt myself falling, and for a second, I thought that this was it. It was my time to meet the Lord.

I hope there are cats in heaven.

Luckily for me, the carpeted stairwell had a four-foot landing halfway up where the stairs took a forty-five-degree turn, and that was the exact spot I landed flat on my back. *Oof.* I gasp for air with eyes as wide as baseballs. Pain shot through my spine, but the air… I needed air.

"What the heck just happened!" My mom screams as her eyes land on me squirming in pain on the stairs. "Ruby! Oh my goodness. Are you okay? What were you thinking?"

I winced up to a seated position with her help, and I began to rub my back where it hurt the most. Blood was seeping through my shirt by my left rib, and I examined its stain on my hand in shock. My dad took the stairs two at a time, scooped me up off the ground, and carried me to the couch. Every step he'd taken with me in his arms felt more and more like torture. Dad, Mom, Charleigh, and Dad's boss—I think his name is Bug—stood in front of me in shock. I was in too much pain and way too embarrassed to cry. I swallowed hard.

Here I go again, messing up as always.

They think I'm a joke.

Why do I always prove them right?

"I'm so sorry, Buzz," my dad turned to his boss, and my face reddened. I *felt* his disappointment.

"No worries, Russ. I have a little guy at home that fell out of a tree just last week. I get it. I'll just see you in the morning. Thanks for having me for dinner, Jade!" My mom nodded, and he excused himself from the tense living room and out the front door and into the night.

I wish I could go with him.

Hotels always have the best breakfast buffets.

"Ruby Leigh Brooks." He shook his head, annoyed. "What in the world would possess you to run into the banister? You could've really hurt yourself! You're lucky you just got the wind knocked out of you."

I didn't feel lucky at the moment.

"I'm sorry," I said to them as my head sank to my chest. My back hurt but not as much as this little family meeting did. It's déjà vu all over again. I seemed to be the center of these discussions often.

"You're gonna have to stop being so reckless, Ruby," my mom scolded me. "One of these days, your impulsivity's gonna catch up with you."

"Yes, Mom. I'll do better," I say out of obligation, but in my mind, my fingers were crossed behind my almost-broken back.

I can't be careful.

Careful is boring.

And I'm NOT boring.

Lightning cracks and brings me back to the present situation. I *have* to find my parents. I look down the foyer to the front door, and to my surprise, it's wide open. The midnight air is thick with electricity, and a chill runs through my veins. I look around the darkness.

Did the wolves follow me?

I shake my head as if to clear the beasts away like an Etch A Sketch. When my eyes adjust, I only see my parents.

Dad is seated on the front stoop with his knees spread slightly apart. Mom's small frame is melted into his, and her head is slightly resting on his shoulder while her soft brown hair blows like the leaves on the trees. I can only see the back of them, but the sweet scene stops my mission.

They look like the boy and his tree.

A sudden flash makes me fall back from the broken railing, and my bum thuds on the scratchy carpet. This house isn't that old, but the carpet has taken a beating with two active girls running up and down the hallway for six years. From my newfound perch, I see Mom grab Dad's hand in preparation for the aftermath of the strike. My dad lifts his arm to pull my mom closer into him, and I get a pang of jealousy.

I wish I was sitting in between them.

It looks safe.

I feel the skin on my arms stretch as my chest goes in and out, and the blood begins to flow back to my fingers after I loosen my grip. As I watch them sit in silence, a wave of emotion builds up in my throat just like the time I tried not to cry when Ace pushed me down on the playground headfirst, and my mouth got sand and dirt all in it. My nickname was *Sandy* for the rest of the year.

Stupid boys.

But this emotion feels different than that. I'm watching my parents hug, but my heart is sad, like big sad.

It makes no sense.

My stomach is in a knot.

"Russell, how could you do this to us?"

"Jade—"

"No, no." I waited for her to say something else, but she left the *no* as final as she does when I ask to take Bitty Kitty to school. That kind of silence scares me, the kind that comes after someone is done with the tricks and games you are playing and stand up and tell you to buzz off. I wonder if kids ever say "buzz off" to Dad's boss Buzz. That would stink.

But that voice she's using, it's familiar. It's the voice she uses when she's done with Dad's tricks and games.

What did Daddy do to us?

There's an uneasiness in the air that scares me more than the lightning, and I feel the goose bumps pop up in waves over my body. I take one last look at them. I think, *See, Ruby. They're guarding the door. No lighting can get you here*, and that is enough to entice me to go to bed without bothering them. I tiptoe back to my room and slip back under my covers. I scan the sheets for the familiar soft texture of my blankie, and Bitty Kitty jumps up at the foot of my bed and settles between my legs. His purr is like a comfort massage that calms my heart. I'm thankful he's with me.

Wolves can't stand cats.

*****

When I wake up, the hole that Bitty Kitty burrowed is still there with a ring of gray fur, but he's gone. The sun peeks through the curtains, and I'm thankful I made it through the night. Every sunrise means hours and hours before I have to face the dark again.

I hop out of bed and bound down the stairs to investigate the pantry. If no one's up yet, I get free rein of the snacks, and I can hide the papers in the bottom of the trash can. *Pop-Tarts are not a nutritious breakfast, Ruby,* her voice echoes in my head. She's on a diet. She's always on a diet with her friends. They will sit around the McDonald's table sipping black coffee, while we kids run the Play Place at the mall. All she eats now is cottage cheese on tomatoes with salt and pepper.

Gross.

I'll never eat cottage cheese.

As I grab the side of the doorway and swing myself into the den, I stop abruptly when I see Charleigh sitting on the couch across from Mom and Dad.

Darn.

No Pop-Tarts.

I guess that it's gonna be oatmeal this morning. At least she lets me put brown sugar in it. Charleigh likes hers plain like Mom.

"Have a seat, Ruby. We need to talk."

That is never good.

I'm not hungry anymore.

I look at Charleigh for answers, but she looks just as confused as me. Dad is cupping his face in his hands, and his hair is disheveled. I know he's been running his hands through it back to front in frustration like he does when I don't listen the first time. I walk slowly around the couch and scoop up Bitty Kitty on my way, and I slide in a bit too close to Charleigh, but she doesn't protest.

Mom is sitting stoically as she always does. Her posture is always on point. I love to feel her soft skin with my fingers. I always wonder if my skin will be as soft as hers one day.

She breaks the silence. "Your dad and I have something to tell you." I dart my eyes to meet Charleigh's, and she's in a blank stare.

"Russell, how could you do this to us?"

Dad is still staring at the ground. Bitty Kitty makes his escape, and I wish I could run out of the room with him.

"Dad and I love you very much." She grabs a tissue from the side table and dabs at the corner of her eye. I don't see any tears, but her face looks as if it could crumble at any second. I shift my weight toward Charleigh, and she grabs my hand and holds it tightly.

Does she know something I don't?

"Do you know what a divorce is, Ruby?" I'm surprised that my mom is directing the question at me, and I hear my dad let a whimper out as he tries to choke back tears.

"No."

My answer came out wrong.

"Well, it's when two people who are married decide to—"

"No!"

She stops.

I *do* know what divorce is. A girl in my kindergarten class was sent to the counselor because her parents got divorced. Her dad moved to California immediately after she found out. Now she only gets to see him on Thanksgiving and every other Christmas. I always hear her quietly praying to God for them to get married again before she eats lunch. I didn't even know that parents had the option to not be married, and it upset me. When I got home from school, I went straight to Dad.

I remember he was cutting the grass, and I waved him down with both arms so he would *know* it was serious, and he stopped the self-propelled mower that Pop had bought him last Christmas. Pop was always buying us new things. I think he wanted Mom to have nice things like she had when she was growing up. They lived in a HUGE house. I liked to play on the staircase when we visited. It is fancy like the hotel downtown we ate at on Mom's birthday. It's pretty and all, but big houses aren't for me—too many places for wolves to hide.

The flailing arms worked, and he redirected his path and turned off the motor when he got a few feet from me. "Goodness, Ruby Leigh. What's up?

"Dad, my friend at school said her parents are getting a divorce. Her dad is moving to California, and she'll only see him like twice a year."

He whipped the sweat from his brow with his neon-pink cutoff shirt. His skin was always so tan. He used to be a lifeguard in Delaware. I always loved picturing him running down the sand to save a kid from drowning.

He offered, "Yes, Ruby, it's sad when people call it quits in their marriage, especially when kids are involved, really sad."

"Will you and Mom ever get divorced?"

Please say no, please say no.

He pulled me into a sweaty, wet embrace, and he clutched my head firmly to his chest. He smelled like freshly cut grass and laundry detergent. I closed my eyes and waited for him to speak.

"Ruby Leigh, your mom and I love each other very much. We will *never* get a divorce. You hear me?" His hug tightened. "Never. I promise."

He promised.

I think about that conversation as I sit here listening to Mom say the unspeakable words.

"No!" I repeat as loudly as I can without bursting into tears. They're coming up in my throat like that day on the playground or that night on the stairs, but I choke them out. They won't listen to me if I'm crying. They need to know I mean business. "You can't get a divorce!" I wiggle out of Charleigh's grasp and fall at Dad's feet. I rip his hands off his face and look desperately into his blue eyes rippled with red veins from crying. "Dad, you promised. You promised."

He pulls me into his lap and hugs me close as I hear his breath break as he sucks in deeply. "I know, Ruby, I know. Your Mom and I...we—"

I whip around to look at Mom. She's still sitting up straight with the tissue wrung around her thumb so hard that the color leaves her fingertip. She's not crying. She is silent.

"Russell, how could you do this to us?"

I look back to Dad, and he softly holds my gaze as his lip quivers.

"Why?" Her question hits like a glass dropped on the tile, and Mom moves across the room and pulls Charleigh onto her lap. She's rhythmically wiping the tears that are pouring down her cheeks. The whole transition feels stiff and forced because neither Mom nor Charleigh are very affectionate people.

"Well, honey, your dad and I have decided that we are just better off friends." She takes a deep breath and lifts her chin a bit higher, and I see a single tear escape from her eye and make its way to her mouth. She wipes it from her lips with the tissue, and I feel Dad's body begin to shake.

Friends?

Don't they have friends?

Bid? Peggy? Rita? Lee?

Those are friends.

Mom and Dad are supposed to be married, not friends!

So many questions enter my mind. Will dad move out? Will he move to California? Will I go with him? What about Charleigh? Will we stay together, or will one of us go with Dad and the other with Mom? What about my birthday? My party is next week! Will we still have it? The ponies are coming, and so are all my friends. Are there still birthdays in divorce? Thanksgiving? Christmas? My head is spinning.

I should have run with Bitty Kitty.

As if she can read my mind, Mom tries to reassure us, "Charleigh, Ruby, we'll always be your parents, and we'll always be here for you. It just may look different from now on. Your dad is moving in with your uncle, and you'll be able to see him anytime you want."

I can feel Dad's chest heaving, but no sound escapes his lips. He musters up the words, "I love you girls more than anything, more than *anything*. Nothing can change that."

Mom stands up and states plainly, "Russell, I'll be in my room. I'll let you wrap things up with the girls."

And just like that, the (last) family meeting ended. Charleigh and I look at each other and then both of our eyes land on Dad. He musters up a smile through the tears, and he gestures to Charleigh to come join me in his lap. He squeezes us so tight that I'm having a hard time breathing, but the suffocation felt welcoming. My heart hurt so bad that any other pain was more tolerable than the pain from realizing that my family would never be the same.

After that day, the wolves no longer only came out at night.

CHAPTER 4

Sunday, October 17, 2021

Sunday

The birds are chirping more than normal in the afternoon sun, and I know they're giving me the business. I've failed to fill their feeder for the second day in a row. Yesterday I was busy with the party prep and kid chaos, and today? Today is one of those days that if I move, I break, and I can't afford to break.

Michael's still MIA. I turned off my phone after I didn't hear anything from him by lunchtime.

If it's off, I won't know if he's ghosting me.

Fear of rejection, rule 101: if you don't care, you don't hurt.

Hudson and Nali are alternating doing flips on the trampoline, and Murphie's purrs are almost as loud as the finches' complaints. She's curled up tighter than a sushi roll, and her fur is hot as a fireball, making my legs sweat under my jeans. I feel uncomfortable, but feeling anything other than broken is welcome at the moment.

Since I was a kid, I always wanted to stand out, blend in, and disappear all at the same time. Like a beautiful tapestry that hangs in an eccentric mountain-town sidewalk shop that makes you stop and wonder how a human's hands so perfectly put together such an imperfect masterpiece, yet you could never imagine it hanging in your own living room. That's how I envisioned myself: unique, beautiful, intriguing, but most likely not for you.

I remember wanting to be wanted so badly but then being terrified of actually being chosen. Being chosen came with the risk that at some point, you could be unchosen, and that, my friends, is never fun. It seems my life's been one big oxymoron so far, an antithesis of contradictions that when woven together, it creates the rift between wisdom and disorder in my brain.

I'm exhausted, but I refuse to ask for help.

I love being around people, but their energy drains me completely.

I'm an open book, but the dark corners of my mind are the silent killers.

I'm hungry for life but still struggle to accept that I have a right to feed myself.

I want a deep, trusting connection, but I struggle to accept anyone's love.

I don't trust anyone, and then I put ALL my trust someone, and yet again I'm left out in the cold to fill the archetype of "dumb girl that never learns."

I know I'm not the only one who feels this way, but I'm the only one experiencing my own two-faced existence, and I can't even stand to be in my own presence; sometimes, I can really suck.

Is it possible to ghost yourself?
Check, please.

The coronavirus hit the world like an F5 tornado, yet the breakdown of so many marriages after the lockdown still burns like a tragic California wildfire. In the past year and a half, I've watched marriage after marriage around me crumble, and my intuition and desperation were once again at odds. I thought Michael and I were in the best place we've ever been, and yet I still felt a sickness in my belly that told me to *beware*. Since slow starvation is no longer an option, my anxieties have manifested in fishing for reassurance from Michael, and I've hated myself for it. Yet again, life has proven over and over again to me that I'm not the exception to the rule.

Turns out, neither is my marriage.

I thought it was.

*****

It's 9:30 p.m.—lunches packed, teeth brushed, prayers said, songs sang, and kisses given. It's finally time for a glass of wine and a joint. I used to judge the hell out of people that took meds and smoked, but it turns out that CBD flower, Prozac, and talk therapy are the trifecta that allow me to joyfully function as a human being, so why would I continue to deny my body of its primal right to peace? I did that with food and exercise for half my life already, so I refuse to sit and suffer to make the mainstream mama's around me comfortable. Do these vices have repercussions in the long run? Yes. Does living with anxiety and chaos within my core actually count as a life? Not one bit.

Cheers.

"Champagne Supernova" drones on the speaker just loud enough to drown out the slow traffic in the distance. I lean back in the rocking chair and wrap my throw blanket around me a little tighter. I regret not bringing my weighted one out. I take a drag, hold my breath as long as I can, and let the smoke trickle out of my nostrils at its will. I give it a final push into the night, and I wash the tang of the flower down with a sip of wine. My phone is stagnant on the table next to me, begging me to touch it like the puff paint sweatshirts my mom always crafted in the 80's. I don't want to take on the stain of temptation, but is a Scarlet Letter that bad?

What if he hasn't texted?

What if he hasn't called?

I was willing to take the chance.

I grabbed the phone and turned it on. The familiar apple that I remember from the rainbow desktop days pops up, and I type in our passcode. Yes, we have the same passcode. Yes, we know all of each other's passcodes. Hell, he's set up ninety percent of my accounts! Why? Because we trust each other.

*Trusted.

My home screen pops up, and it's one of my favorite pictures of our family. We are all in our mountain clothes, comfy and snuggly, smooshed together on Mom's back porch in the North Carolina twilight. My head is resting on Michael's shoulder, and Hudson and I have the same exact close-lipped, content grin, while Nali and Michael are both smiling with their whole face. I stare at the smiles until three notifications pop up: one missed call, one voice mail, and one text message.

Missed call: Michael, 8:00 p.m.

He called before bedtime.

Text: "*Please let me prove to you that I'm worthy of your love.*"

Worthy of my *love?* Our *love?* The love he so carelessly pressed pause on long enough to let sexual thoughts of *my best friend* seep in until the fantasy is so clear and the urge is so great that you can't stop yourself from acting on it? Can that really be *love?* Is it? Because I don't know anymore. Maybe I've never known true love. Maybe there's no such thing. Maybe we're all as idiotic as the iconic couple Romeo and Juliet and will jump into any human connection no matter what the cost just to not die sad and alone. Society is just the classic definition of insanity, and trying to fit in the cookie-cutter molds that we as humans deem right and wrong will send you to an early grave in one way or another.

I take a final hit, exhale, and place the rest of the joint to its stone casing. I remember the voice mail and make a few clicks on the phone, and it begins to play.

"Hey, babe, I just wanted to call and say goodnight to the kids, so, um, I guess, hey, Hud! I miss you, buddy. I'm with your favorite papa on the porch petting Sammie. Hear her panting? She just chased a rabbit out of the yard. She's pretty proud of herself. Hope you hit some balls today. Remember, practice tomorrow. Love you, H-Dawg. And Ms. Nali Blue, I hope you and Murphie got some snuggles with Mama today. I wish I was there to snuggle you and Mama. Will you give her a squeeze for me? Please? A biggggg one. I know you rocked it at school, and I'll need an update on the Frickism of the day pronto. I love you, Boo! And Mama, I love you. Hope to talk to you tomorrow. Good night."

I hover my finger over the little red trash can and lightly graze it to test its sensitivity, and it blinked abruptly and immediately disappeared.

Wait!

I bet there's a way to recover it. I can ask Mich—

Right...

Monday

"Are you sure you want to do this today?" Michael asks as I coldly ignore him from the passenger side of his truck. He looks confused, and I want to tell him to join the damn club. He was home when the kids and I walked in the door from school today, and when he held the two of them in a bear hug, my body was begging me to join, but I didn't. Instead, out of nowhere, I insisted we immediately go get me on my own phone plan at Verizon. I didn't add that I'd imagined my escape to the mountains and getting my own phone plan was phase I, but I don't need to get ahead of myself. For now, I just have to get out of this house.

I would go to get it switched on my own, but I'm clueless when it comes to our utilities and random plans. Guess I better get on that along with learning how to work the thermostat, how to change the filters, and…all the things I've gotten comfortable letting him take care of for us. If this marriage is really done, I need to make a list of all the little dealtils of our life that he manages with ease.

Why is he so annoyingly good at managing it all?

I know I'm only torturing myself, but I just can't get the scene out of my mind. I picture Michael walking up to Cam, moving in closer, looking at her with those anticipating eyes, and I see it play out over and over again in my brain while the wolves pace the floor waiting for me to give up.

I'll cut the grass with my teeth before I let my wolves back in.

*****

On a scale of one to ten, my regret may be at level seventeen at the moment. I'm pretty sure that sitting in Verizon is the ninth layer of hell, and Adele's old song "Hello" is mocking me over the crotchety loudspeaker. And to think I literally just told Cam a few weeks ago, "Adele has a new album coming out, but I'm the happiest I've ever been, so it won't hit the same."

I've always been good at manifesting.

I feel numb.

I remind my inner critic that I'm here to switch my phone service because as soon as I can, I'm getting out of this fake, soul-strangling, suburban town and disappearing in the woods. I have always known that the mountains are where I belong, but this situation has definitely propelled those plans forward for me. In the forest, things make sense. The silence is not deafening like the silence of a lonely bedroom. The stillness brings clarity in a way that is impossible to experience in the rat race of life, and I'm so over all of it right now.

This is my nightmare.

Michael is sitting across from me in the store, and his chin is hanging so low on his chest that I think it's actually touching. I'm sure sleeping in the bed of his truck in the driveway was not ideal, and I know him. He didn't sleep but instead beat himself up the whole night. You know what? *Good*. He should have.

And of course, out of all the people who are available to help us out, we're lucky to get the young man who's newly trained. His name is Hassan, and it's his first day on his own. He appreciates our patience while he "figures out the system." No problem, Hassan. Take your time. I will just be sitting here contemplating running out onto Highway 124.

What are we going to tell the kids?

Hassan fumbled with his lanyard and dropped his ID card down the crack of the desk. Poor kid. I was cursing him in my brain while I should be thanking him for actually showing up to work in the middle of a workers shortage.

I'm a jerk.

Sorry, God.

As I shift my unwarranted silent attack on the innocent employee, I notice there is an older man kicking the machine in the corner of the store. *Jerk.* How can he think that is an acceptable way of getting a piece of equipment to work? Then I thought back to the closet-door incident this morning. I hate that freakin' door. It has *never* worked right. I almost break my wrist every time I attempt to close it, and my OCD definitely does not let open be an option. I asked Michael to fix it years ago, along with his inability to connect with anyone, but alas, here we sit.

Good news is, he will have to fix it now because I kicked a hole through it.

Oops.

I suck in a deep breath, and Michael's eyes are locked on mine. I start to offer him a smile, and then I remember myself.

God, please give me a sign.

I could really use one right now…

"All right Mr. and Mrs. Blue," Hassan's timely interruption brings me back to the present moment, and I'm both disgusted and irritated at seeing Michael smile kindly at him. How can he just smile? Right now, I prefer him pouting like my ninth graders when they get that F on the test that they claimed they studied for, but we all know *that's a lie.* "Can you put in your passcodes and unlock the phones, please?" I grab them both and begin hitting the numbers on both of our phones. I was not about to let him do a thing for me.

I don't want to feel so hurt.

A second customer begins wrestling with the broken payment machine in the corner, and I refrain from calling her an asshole in my brain, which I count as growth. She cusses the machine, turns to look for help, and exclaims, "I don't have time for this!" Her mood is relatable.

The woman waiting for assistance sucks her teeth in a "*forget this*" fashion and turns her attention to her peloton workout that's blaring on her phone. The instructor is trying to motivate the overpaying millennials to give it their best effort today, and I giggle at the fact that this woman is watching the workout, but she's not working out. She's kickboxing a machine in Verizon, but she's not working out.

I want to run.

As the workout progresses and she waits, I hear the instructor yell, "*If you want something, you have to work for it! You have to want it deep from within! It's like a good marriage. It takes work...hard work! But it's worth it friends, so keep fighting for what you want, and you can get there!*" and it startles me.

The hairs stand up like cornfields on my forearms.

God, is that you?

"Michael, did you hear that?" He turned his head slowly toward me, knit his brow together, and shook his head.

"No, I didn't." He is always short and timid with his speech when I'm angry. I can be a bit harsh, I suppose, but this time, he deserved it. I didn't even yell at him when I saw him today. However, in his defense, silence and shade from me are much worse.

He may not have heard the sign from the Lord, but I sure did. *Marriage takes work*—hard work. I'm so sick and tired of *working*. We have been through challenges in our marriage in the past, but recently, I've been enjoying the vacation from the chaos. Why'd he have to screw it up?

I've gotta get outta here.

Suddenly, it felt like the walls were closing in on me. I glanced around for an exit plan. "Hassan, do you guys have a bathroom?"

"No, ma'am, we don't."

"Of course you don't." I turned to Michael and said, "I'm going to find a bathroom." He nodded, and I beeline it to the front doors. As I walk into the sun, my face begins to sting. It's rubbed raw from the tears and tissues that have piled on my bedroom floor. I put my hands in my pockets and look around me. It's early fall in Georgia, so it's hot as hell already, and it's only 11:00 a.m. I see that Goodwill is the closest bathroom option, so I reluctantly trudge down the hill into the parking lot. A horn honks and shakes me out of my head, and I wave at the familiar face. I always love seeing parents of students when I look like I have not showered or slept in days.

God help me.

As I approach the front entrance of the store, I hear a booming voice calling on God, and I'm intrigued. I look over to see a middle-aged woman praying over an elderly woman who is melting into her loving embrace. Her eyes are closed, and she is nodding at the words that are being poured over her. It's a beautiful moment that I feel thankful for witnessing. I reluctantly turn and move toward the sliding doors of the entrance, but something forces me to stop.

You asked for help.

I stood right in the entrance just as the sliding door creaked open, and the greeter said, "Good morning. Welcome to Goodwill." I continued to stare into the store without making eye contact with the kind employee. There was a supernatural force that paralyzed me. I need to turn around and listen, but I felt like it would be an intrusion on their moment. Desperation outweighed possible disrespect at this point, so I made the slow turn toward the prayers.

Maybe they aren't for me specifically, but I have never known a person who is willing to pray out loud in a public space to turn away someone that needs to hear the Word. I inch my way awkwardly toward the two women in hopes they would not mind. I wanted a sign, and here it is. I have ignored God prompts before, and I learned if you don't listen when he throws you pebbles, he'll throw rocks. And if you don't pay attention to the rocks, he'll start throwing boulders. Stubborn as I am, I've been hit with many boulders in my life, and I would like to avoid *that* pain at all costs, thank you very much.

As I slowly approach the pair, I see a slow, proud smile curl on the woman's lips who's doing the praying, yet she did not even open her eyes to witness my presence. I take the subtle gesture as my invitation. I fold my hands across my chest, trying to feel a sliver of security, and I close my eyes to truly allow her words to wash over me. I felt the whoosh of air as her hands shot to the sky, and she proclaimed loudly, "God, when two or more gather in your name, you are *here* with us, Lord Jesus. You are here, and we can feel you, God!"

Is it okay to move closer?

Does COVID count in God-prompted moments?

Forget it.

I inch my way into the arms of the two women who organically make room as they break their embrace to include me, and I feel my body begin to shake, and my jaw chatters audibly. It always does that when I'm overcome with emotion. I let my teeth freely clank together as the women continue to summon the power of their higher being.

"This woman, Lord…she's here for a reason, God." His messenger suddenly broke the triangle we'd formed, and she turned and grabbed my face—hard. I open my eyes. Tears are welling up as my jaw relaxes in her strong, loving grip. I'm suddenly overcome with emotion, and I can't stop the tears from pouring over my bottom lids. I don't attempt to wipe them away as she stares deep into my soul with an intensity that almost makes my heart stop.

She begins talking in tongues, and I don't even try to understand or decipher the meaning. I just let the words wash over me as she frames my face by holding my cheeks between her hands. The only time I have ever witnessed someone talking in tongues was years ago in a small Pentecostal church in Corinth, Mississippi, with my college bestie Joanna. I was thoroughly freaked out when the preacher began grabbing a man in the aisle and violently shaking him as he cried and received what seemed like an exorcism in front of one hundred plus strangers. I swore to never attend that church again, and I kept my word. At twenty, I was not yet ready to allow God to penetrate my heart, but here I am now at thirty-seven, outside of a Goodwill, with two complete strangers getting demons cast out of my soul.

Only me.

The earthly angel abruptly moves her hands from my cheeks. Her right hand lands on top of my head, pressing down, while her left hand puts pressure under my chin. I've never been touched *this* intimately by a complete stranger, but the gesture feels necessary, and I allow myself to relax into her palms. She repeats the action of holding my face between her hands to cupping the top of my head and the bottom of my chin while she chants, "God, cast the demons from this child, Lord!" I feel her power as she grasps my cheeks once more, almost slapping me in the process, and her intense eyes demand my complete attention.

I'm listening.

"Honey, you are going to be the generational change in your family." She almost sings this declaration as her head flies back, and she lifts her hands to the sky. She let out a guffaw that I imagined came from a deep connection with him, as if he had just whispered to her, "*Yes, my child, that's exactly what she needs to hear.*" How else could she have known?

She shakes me out of my head as she cups my jaw with one hand and thrusts her free palm to the sky and declares, "Jesus, this woman *will* be the change. She's strong, Lord, God. Oh she's so strong. Almighty, we're here, we're here to surround this woman with your love, your light, your hope!"

Her attention shifts from my face to my chest abruptly as her free hand lands hard over my heart. The jolt of this act startles me, but I lift my hands to push her palm deeper into my breast because I don't want there to be a bit of space between her hand and my soul. I can *feel* God. The elder woman is chanting next to us with her arms stretched to the heavens. "Thank you, Jesus. Thank you!" A stifled sob escapes my lips with a force that I was not expecting.

How does she know.

I pause and allow it all to sink in. A man walks past us with his young daughter, and he gently directs her to the opposite side of him away from our circle. Even though the little girl is being dragged into the store, her gaze catches mine, and I give her a smile.

Don't be afraid.

This is a beautiful moment, even if your dad can't see it.

The woman's hand is still firmly, lovingly pressed on my chest, and I lock eyes with her. This messenger, with one sentence, pinpointed the *exact* personal journey that I have been dedicated to ever since I left home years ago, and I crumble into her embrace.

How did she know? How did she know that I needed to hear that one statement more than anything? I repeat it to myself and allow the words to drip down my body like rain.

You are going to be the generational change in your family.

I slowly emerge from the messenger's bosom and roughly wipe my face with the back of my sleeve. Snot and salty tears soak my forearm, and the older woman hands me a tissue from her pocketbook. With a smile and a squint, I graciously accept the Kleenex and work on cleaning myself up as best as I can. Another customer passes the three of us, and not one of us is phased by the interruption.

Thank you, God.

Thank you.

Now that my snot and tears are all collected in the tissue and I can speak without sobs, I ask, "What is your name, ma'am?"

Her chest broadened, and her chin and nose poised themselves in a power pose that Brené would be proud of and declared, "My name's Regina. Regina Love!"

I gently reach for Regina's hands, clasp them in mine, and pull them to my heart. I make sure that she feels my sincerity when I confess, "What you said to me is exactly what I needed to hear." My voice cracks, and I pull back suddenly, feeling the presence of the Goodwill crowd steadily trekking past us on a mission to shop, paying us only a fraction of attention as I fight back the tears once more. I feel exposed. I feel seen. I feel hope. I take a deep breath as Regina pulls me in for one last embrace.

"Oh, child, God gave me the words. He told me loud and clear, and I will never disobey a prayer prompt from my Father." She reaches into her handbag and pulls out a white, black, and red postcard-sized advertisement with a group of stunning women posing like queens on the front. Their hair is long, flowing, and fabulous, and I see the bold cursive print that reads, "Regina Love's Hair Boutique and Salon." I clutched the postcard lovingly, thankful to have a memento from this bizarre but beautiful interaction, and she suddenly rips me from her chest and holds me at arm's length.

"And you can always find me online, honey! Look me up. Regina Love, *The Voice*: season 9, Team Blake all-the-way!"

I blinked my eyes a handful of times to help my brain process the plot twist she just threw into the mix.

"Oh, yeah, girl. I was the one that told Gwen to marry Blake! I called that relationship from a mile away! Regina knows love!" she proclaimed proudly, and I wanted to tell her that the pun was not lost on me, but I could only muster a smile. All of the sudden, my bladder reminds me of my purpose for the Goodwill trek, and I depart the pair by saying, "You really don't know how much this moment means to me. Thank you." I bowed to Regina Love and the older woman, whose name I didn't even catch. As the doors opened and the smell of Goodwill filled my nostrils, I walked toward the bathroom with a lightness that I did not have ten minutes ago.

Back in Verizon, I sit down next to Michael, and he looks at my fresh cry face with confusion and concern. I look at my watch. I was gone a good twenty minutes. "Are you okay?" he questions. "What happened?"

Not yet ready to let him in on the beauty of the interaction with the strangers who are now forever in my heart, I simply said, "If I told you, you wouldn't believe me." And I looked at Hassan and said, "Do you have the iPhone 13 in white?"

He looked terrified and quickly remarked, "Sure, Mrs. Blue, whatever you would like."

I folded my hands in my lap and gave him a half smile. It was the first time my lips had curled upward since Saturday night. Only I could have demons cast out of me by a hometown celebrity who belted out "Midnight Train to Georgia" on national television.

It's confirmed. I looked her up.

CHAPTER 5

Saturday, October 13, 2001

I raced from room to room in the house, making sure nothing embarrassing was left lying around. Marco's house is always immaculate, so I always feel pressure to clean up our chaos when he comes over. Our house is not trashed. There's just no clear boundaries set on where things belong and where things are actually placed. For example, I've not seen the dining room table since 1999. It's completely covered in bills and paperwork for God knows what, and I can never tell if the clothes in front of the washing machine are clean or dirty. There are shoes in the coat closet that pile up to my chest, so we put the coats on the towel hangers in the bathroom. I do know one thing, though: my room is off-limits to any unwanted or unplanned crap. I can't stand clutter. I feel like it weighs me down.

I like to feel weightless.

I picked up Naomi's tag blankie that Mom left on the couch. *She's gonna regret forgetting this at bedtime tonight!* I take the stairs by two, open Naomi's door, and toss it on her bed. I'm so thankful Mom decided to take her up to the mountain house this weekend. I mean, don't get me wrong, I love my little sister more than anything, but I have plans for tonight that require a certain atmosphere, you know? *Dawson's Creek* meets *One Tree Hill* style!

My mission?

Get on good terms with Marco again.

Everything has to be perfect.

I go to my room to set the mood. Candles? *Check.* Tom Petty's greatest hits? *Check.* Protection? *Double check.* I look at my cloud bedspread and the stenciled stars adorning the walls and cringe a bit. Marco helped me paint them when we first began dating in seventh grade, but in the candlelight, they feel so juvenile.

Oh well.

Nothing I can do now.

I remove the stuffed animals off my bed and replace them with the throw pillows that I took from Charleigh's room. She would kill me if she knew I borrowed them, especially for a romantic night with Marco. I look around.

It's as good as it can be.

Since Mom and Naomi's dad, Tim, got divorced, it's been just we girls in the house. She met Tim soon after her divorce with my dad was finalized, and he wooed her with elaborate trips across the world. Tim Simpson was a farming mogul, just like her dad, and she and Charleigh loved the fancy life that we lived when we were a part of the Simpson household. I hated it with a passion.

A different set of wolves came with the money.

I felt like an outsider watching a romantic movie unfold, but as happy as I was for the main character to be wined and dined, I was left feeling forgotten along with the remnants of her former life.

Tim had two boys who were younger than Charleigh and me by a few years, and the youngest was not bad, but even thinking about the shit that the older boy pulled makes me feel sick to my stomach today. I can still hear the squeal of the metal spinning as he drilled a peephole in my wall from the bathroom to gawk at me while I was changing. As many times as I tried to fill the hole in, another would appear in a discrete location in hopes I wouldn't figure it out. I finally ended up bringing duct tape with me from my dad's house to block his vision, but the point was moot. He'd just drill through the tape too.

I was only nine years old.

One time, Charleigh and the two boys tricked me into playing potato sack race through the upstairs of the massive house. They convinced me that the duct tape I took from my dad's was more stable than Mom's nice pillowcases, but I felt instant regret as I heard the screech of the tape and felt the constraint of the almost indestructible material around my ankles. As the older boy and I began racing down the hallway, Charleigh popped out of the guest bedroom as we hopped past and proceeded to shove me butt first into a laundry basket. They worked as a pair. She and the devil's spawn hog-tied my wrists, bound my ankles, duct-taped my mouth shut, and then dragged me into the toilet closet, where the littlest boy had just taken a *massive shit*. They pushed the basket right next to the poop-filled bowl and then slammed the door behind them. I was stuck, trapped with no way to escape or call for help. My mother found me forty-five minutes after bedtime, and all the other kids were dutifully asleep in their rooms. She scolded me for being so reckless with my ridiculous games, and grounded me for the entire next week.

I cried, begged, and pleaded for her to believe me. "*They tricked me! They set me up!*" But not one of them, not even Charleigh, confessed that they were the masterminds of the operation. Here I was, one again, the delinquent, anxious child that continued to muddy up the pristine waters of my mother's shiny new life. I was given the role of "the joke" before I knew what a punch line actually was.

It's over, Ruby.

You are not in that toxic environment anymore.

I stop for a second to take a look at myself in the hallway mirror.

Gross.

I knew I should've skipped lunch.

Marco and I have been together since seventh grade in 1998. He was the new kid who moved to Georgia from upstate Oregon, and we ended up in the same seventh grade homeroom. He was European, tall, lanky, and cute as hell with a big smile full of braces. He was into sports, so he fit in perfectly with my clique of rec-park-roaming friends. He ended up being the quarterback for the team that year, and it was a big honor for our little crew to claim such a coveted position. Marco set his sights on me early, and I was never mad at the attention he was always willing to give.

By the time we reached high school, Marco and I were in full-blown puppy love. He had a way with words, and his smooth-talking charm and increasingly good looks made my teenage heart explode on the daily. He walked me to every class, and he would always slip me a note under the door of my bio class on his way to lunch. He even asked me to homecoming with a scavenger hunt that was set up all over town! By the time we were sixteen, we were acting like an old married couple, spending every second we could together, and any time we could get *"alone" alone*, even better.

God, we have such an intense connection.

It was really easy to get that alone time on my end. With Mom going to the mountain house any chance she could get, it left our house empty often. Charleigh and I worked out a way to split the time at the house on the weekends she was away with Naomi, and it's worked in our favor so far...

Until the prank war started.

One time, Marco and I were in my bed, fooling around when Mom was gone, and Charleigh and her boyfriend, Robert, decided to drive by and hit the garage door opener for fun. Oh, I remember it being really fun...for them!

One time, we were in the middle of a heavy petting make-out session, and we heard the garage door rumble like thunder in the distance. The way it makes the house shake when it opens is always our warning that someone is coming, and we both simultaneously jump out of the bed. We struggled clumsily to get our clothes back on quickly, and Marco almost fell down the stairs as his athletic legs floated him over the banister while he was still buckling his jeans at a full sprint.

As soon as we got to the bottom of the stairs, the garage door began to shut again, and I opened the front door to investigate. I saw Robert's teal Civic speeding down the street, and I vaguely made out Charleigh's head thrown back in fits of laughter in the passenger seat. They got us.

Assholes.

It's fine, though. I got them back. The next week, when it was her turn to have the house for her shenanigans, I left an anonymous tip to our nosy neighbor that someone was parked illegally in the street, and she called the HOA president. Charleigh got slapped with a one-hundred-dollar ticket that Mom made her pay with her own money.

To quote Matt Damon in Good Will Hunting, *"How 'bout them apples!"*

But back to tonight, it *has* to go perfectly, so I gave Charleigh gas money to stay away. Marco has been getting on to me about my eating habits lately, and I'm afraid he is getting over it. When I say *it*, I mean me. I can't lose him. I have to smooth things out tonight.

I need him.

I wish I could say our problem was as simple as the archetypal popular girl's boyfriend-stealing habits, but it is a bit more complicated than a pair of fake-tan legs, Uggs, and Daisy Dukes. Marco got deep into bodybuilding after he was booted from the varsity quarterback position his sophomore season. He had a few bad games, and the coach just tossed him like a bad habit. He's been training for a national teen competition for over a year now, and his rigid exercise and eating routine takes precedence to everything and over everyone in his life. I mean, I'm all about his abs—don't get me wrong—but he began to take things to extremes.

About three months ago, we were sitting in the Wendy's drive-through line, and a crackling voice came over the loudspeaker, "Can I take your order?" I lean across Marco from the passenger side and hold myself up by putting my hands on his thighs, and he kisses my neck as I giggle through the order.

"I'll have the side salad. No dressing, please, and water with that." I turn my head to receive the kisses on my mouth. He shoots me a straight-tooth grin flashing how well the braces worked.

He pulls back and says, "Get a burger!"

A burger?

Hell no.

What's he thinking?

"Scratch the salad," he interjects. "She will have a number one, double, add bacon, and a Coke."

He knows I don't eat red meat. Ever since "mad cow disease" hit the US, my mom refused to buy red meat and has strongly encouraged us not to eat it. The only unhealthy thing in our pantry is a box of stale reduced-fat Oreos, and those are just for Naomi when she eats all her vegetables. My mom's motto is that one should eat to live, not live to eat, and the amount of organic vegetables and lack of any processed food in the house supports her beliefs. I seem to be the only one that actually likes junk food, but I stopped eating anything like that a while back. I have to fit into the size zero Seven7 jeans that I just bought.

"Relax, Ruby. I have a way that you can eat this *and* stay fit." He winks and ruffles my hair.

Eat this and stay fit?

How?

When the food is passed to us from the window, Marco hands it all to me and pulls onto the road, one hand on the wheel and the other on the clutch. The food in my lap is hot, and it is making me anxious as the overwhelming smell of french fries fills my nostrils.

"Why do you look so pale, Rube? You know a burger sounds *way* better than a dressingless salad." He grabs the straw and stabs the Coke with a swift motion, and he slurps the drink aggressively.

"It's just—" I start, and he slams the Coke in the cup holder and turns the radio up louder. I yell over the noise, "It's just weird. That's all."

"What do you mean?" He turns his big brown eyes to meet mine, and his brows lift waiting for a reply.

What am I supposed to say here? I'm so confused. He is in the middle of training for this competition. He made me swear that I would go on a strict diet with him of only grilled vegetables and chicken or salad sans the dressing, and we had been sticking to it for months now. We go to the gym before and after school to lift, and I run at least a mile before bed each night. I have already broken the one-meter springboard diving record for the varsity swim team, and I'm seeded to be in the top ten at the state meet in January. My stomach is flatter than Britney Spears's, and I'm even getting attention from other guys.

Maybe that is why he wants me to get fat.

"I just don't see how we can eat like this and still stay on track physically. That's all." I see the grease beginning to seep through the brown sack, and my stomach growls in anticipation. It's been so long since I've eaten a burger, and my mouth is watering to the point that I have to pause and swallow.

It smells really good.

Marco leans over the middle console and grabs my hand and pulls it to his lips. His slow and soft kiss sends shivers down my spine.

I'll do whatever you say. Just promise you will always kiss me like this.

"Look," he starts, "I've found a way to eat what I want but still stay on track with my training."

"Go on," I tease as I run my fingers through his dark hair.

"Well, it's simple. When you eat something that you don't want to gain the calories and fat from, you simply wash it down with a ton of water, and then you throw it right back up." He said it so nonchalantly as he was lacing and unlacing his fingers through mine and playing with the aquamarine promise ring he gave me for my birthday.

"Wait, what?" I was confused. "How do you make yourself throw up? Is that even possible?"

"Oh, for sure. Wrestlers do it all the time to make weight." He continued, "It's not hard at all. I'll show you when we get back to the house."

I pull my hand away from his and begin to pick at my thumbnail.

He'll show me?

And he did. We ate the burger and fries cross legged on my bed while Tim and Faith played in the background. "It's Your Love" was our song, and I made sure to play it any chance I could get. Ketchup dripped off my burger and dropped onto my tan thigh. He took his finger and slowly removed it in a very intentional, pressured motion. He lingered on my skin for a moment, and then reached up so that his finger met my lips. I opened my mouth just enough to let him slide in and I closed my lips around his finger and teased him with the tip of my tongue.

"And it's just like that." He slid his finger from between my lips and then ruffled my hair like he always does.

"Just like what?" I was lost.

"Like that," he repeated. "Come on, Ruby. Don't make me spell it out for you."

I could sense his frustration, so I dropped it.

I'll figure it out myself.

"Remember to drink up. Makes it easier coming up."

So basically, eat desired food, drink lots of fluids, put my finger down my throat, and the rest will work itself out... *literally.*

"Isn't doing this called something? I swear we learned about this in health—" My question is deflected with a glare.

"No, stupid! That's bulimia. This is different. If you just do this every now and again, it won't hurt you. How do you think I'm able to stay so dedicated to the frickin' chicken-and-veg diet? I know that if I slip up and eat something bad, I can get rid of it easily." He takes the last bite of his burger and slurps up the last bit of soda in the bottom of his cup. "Listen, I'll take the downstairs bathroom, and you can do your thing up here." He hopped off my bed, gave me a kiss on the cheek, and was down the stairs in what seemed like three strides.

"*Do my thing?*"

Is this my thing now?

I go into the bathroom, and I lock the door behind me. I turn on the sink to drown out the noise, and walk up to the toilet and stare.

You can eat whatever you want and still not get fat.

I kneel down in front of the toilet and lift the lid slowly. The bowl is disgusting. I was supposed to clean it this weekend, but with Mom gone, there is no one to yell at me to do it. I regretted the lack of effort on my part now. I gathered my long dyed-blond hair into a low ponytail, and as my hands worked the hair tie, I thought about Marco downstairs.

Was he done?

Am I taking too long?

I better get it over with.

I lean my forearms on the rim of the bowl and grab for one last sip of my soda. The liquid feels cool going down, and my stomach is uncomfortably full after finishing the entirety of the meal. I look at the water and slowly bring my pointer finger to my mouth, just as Marco had done with his. I let my finger slide past the hangy ball in the back of my throat, and I instantly gagged and gripped the bowl with white knuckles.

Nothing happened.

I repeated the action one more time, and again, I gagged, but nothing else came up.

Am I doing it right?

Maybe if I use two fingers…

I added my middle finger to the mission, and that did the trick. With my top teeth scraping my knuckles, I shoved the two finger in with such force that I was surprised by the recoil of my stomach as a warm hash of burger, fries, and Coke came flooding out of my mouth and all over my hand that I did not remove fast enough. The vomit hit the water with such force that it splashed up and hit me in the face.

Damn.

That was crazy.

I grabbed desperately for the toilet paper next to me, and I began scraping the puke off the back of my hand and wiping the backsplash of toilet water off my face. I tossed the used tissue on top of the throw up, and I sat back to look at my work.

That was surprisingly easy.

I inspected the pile, and I determined that once was not enough, so I repeated the process three more times until I had nothing left to purge. I felt satisfied. I felt powerful. I felt strong. I had discovered the secret to having my cake and eating it too—*literally.*

I walked to the sink and scrubbed my hands over and over with soap. I picked my toothbrush out of the cup, and I was extra generous when putting on the toothpaste. I heard a creak in the floor, and I turned to see Marco doing his best James Dean impression in the doorway. I give him a closed-lip smile as I continue to scrub the bad taste out of my mouth.

"You have an extra one of those for me?" I reach to the second drawer where we keep our old dental goody bags, and I toss him a hot pink one with a wink. "My favorite color!" he declared and ripped the package open and grabbed the toothpaste in one swoop. "So how did it go?"

He turned to catch my gaze in the mirror. His expression is flat, and I suddenly feel exposed. I spit the foam into the sink and turned the water on to wash my evidence down the drain.

"Went fine." I shrug.

He nodded and spit in the sink I just cleaned. He tossed the toothbrush down, turned and walked through the door, and then plopped on my bed. I turn the water back on and wash his mess away. I watched as the sink cleared, and I wiped my hands and caught my own reflection in the mirror. I noticed that my cheeks were swollen from the purging, and my mascara was running in the corner of my left eye. I took a deep breath.

That was really easy.

But why are the wolves pacing?

The clock chiming in the hall brings me back to the present. It's eight thirty, and he should be here any time. I apply the lip gloss he likes and place it on the counter for later. I'm hoping that we will mess it up the fun way this time instead of with tissues and tears.

God, please let this go well.

"Knock, knock!" he said as he let himself in the front door and locked it behind him.

"Hey, handsome!" I sang, and I skipped over to him and jumped in his arms. I easily wrapped my legs around his waist as my hands combed through his hair. I leaned in slowly for a kiss then jutted my face to the right, dropped my arms to the ground, and ungracefully wiggled my way out of his grasp.

He loves when I resist.

I dove onto the couch, and he was close behind ready to pounce. As he flew through the air to meet me on the cushions, I rolled left before he could reach me and landed flat-backed on the floor. He pushed up off the couch and landed in a plank position right above me and chaturanga-style lowered himself on top of me.

"Got you," he whispered as he kissed behind my ear.

I grabbed his hips and pulled them to where they dug into mine. I feel him adjust himself and then begin to finger the button of my Abercrombie jeans. His other hand is making its way up my stomach, and he stops when he hits my ribs, and he lifts his head to face me.

"What's up with this?" He ran his fingers up and down the ridges of my rib cage like he was playing a glissando, and then his hand landed on my sharply protruding hip bone. He squeezed it hard, and I recoiled in pain.

"Ouch, Marco! That hurt!" I yelp as I roll out from under him. I sat up and wrapped my arms around my stomach and rubbed my sore pelvis.

"Well, damn, Ruby. I'm not surprised that it hurts. You have zero fat on your body. It's disgusting, for real. Are you still throwing up? I told you to quit that shit. I'm serious!"

You're the one that taught me how to do it, Marco.
Remember that?

I stand up, stomp toward the kitchen, and grab my lip gloss and reapply. I didn't need it, but I did need to move. I look at him with an accusing glare, and he snaps.

"Ruby, don't you even put this shit on me. I see that look. Listen, I told you to do it *every once in a while,* not every time you eat!"

He gets up and walks toward me with a look that is a combination of both anger and sadness. He gets within inches of me and puts his hands around my waist. He squeezes his grip around me and tries to make his fingers touch on both sides. His hands are strong, and it hurts all the way through to my spine. I duck out of his grip and dart for the bathroom.

I feel him close on my heels, and our feet squeak on the wood floor as we both shift left into the hallway bath. He is blocking the door with his foot before I can even have a chance to close it, and I back up until my butt hits the sink. I grab it for stability, and my heart feels like it may beat out of my chest. Marco has gotten rough with me before, but this time, it feels different.

God, help me.

He lets out a laugh and says, "Who the hell are you running from?"

"You, asshole," I scoff. I want to say more, but fear stops me from making a sound.

"Listen, Ruby, this has gone far enough. Skinny is the goal, but this…" He shook his head and scrunched up his face as if he just smelled his little brother's socks. "This is way too far. What do you weigh now, ninety pounds?"

Ninety-four, jerk.

"You're five-foot-five, Ruby. This is just not healthy." He spat, and then he grabbed me by the arms and spun me around to face the mirror. He held my head between his hands like he was trying to set up for a free throw, and he forced my face forward. "Look at yourself. *Look!* Your face is sunken in, your eyes are always bloodshot, and you have absolutely no ass anymore. Damn, Ruby. You need to stop."

Tears were building in my eyes, and my teeth started chattering.

"See!" He pointed at me and accused, "You are so fucking tiny that you're freezing in a heated bathroom!" He exploded in one swift motion and grabbed my face and pulled it to his. I could see him fighting back tears too, and his hands were shaking. I let out a whimper, and he pushed my head away from him hard. Marco threw himself on the ground in front of the toilet and began jamming his fingers violently down his throat. Tears were blurring my vision at this point, and I put my hands on my knees, and the tears fell to the ground around my feet.

"Is this what you need to fucking see?" he yelled as he continued to gag himself.

"Stop it, Marco! Just stop!" I was too scared to move, so I allowed myself to sink into the floor for stability.

Please stop.

75

"You don't want to see me throw my life up in the toilet, huh? Is that it? Well, Ruby, that's what you're making me watch you do! I can't do it anymore. I'm out." He slowly got up off the floor, shook the saliva from his fingertips in one swift flick, and stepped over my crumpled body to exit the bathroom. He slammed the front door with a finality that I felt in my soul.

No.

Come back.

*****

I reluctantly walked into the school Monday morning with tired eyes and a sore throat from all the purging. My cheeks are superswollen, and my eyes are struggling to stay open due to only getting a few hours of sleep. I went on a bender Saturday after Marco left. It was different from the disordered episodes I've experienced in the past. I felt *desperate* to turn my body inside out, and there was an animallike madness that kept me searching and searching for more to consume so the release would be that much more exhilarating. I ate anything and everything in sight. Oreos, *gone*. Pop-Tarts, *finished the box*. Milk, *drank every last drop*. I topped it all off with a gallon of ice cream and a side of apples and peanut butter, which I regretted later.

I didn't chew the apples long enough.

The air was thick with speculation, and even my normal acquaintances were avoiding making eye contact with me in the halls.

How does everyone already know?

I make it to my locker, open it with an unnecessary vigor, bury my head into it, and let out the breath that I didn't realize I'd been holding in since the parking lot. There's a potent stink of textbook mixed with Bath & Body Works, and my stomach lurches as the aroma it fills my nostrils and proceeds to hit the back of my throat. I feel the tickle of the bile rising up, and I place my hand over my mouth to attempt to will it back down.

"You okay, sugar?" It was little Mrs. Taylor, my AP Lit teacher. She's no taller than a kindergartener, and her head barely reaches my shoulder as she rubs my back in a circular motion like my Boom-ma used to do.

I lie, "Yes, ma'am. Thank you."

"Where's that boyfriend of yours? He's usually looking like he wants to eat you with a spoon by the time the bell rings every morning!" She nudges my arm and gives me a wink. She's a veteran teacher in her sixties, her kids are grown and gone, and her husband died a few years back, so I think she lives for all the young love radiating through the high school halls. Marco is in her second period, and I'm in her first, so she witnesses our interactions daily, both the good and the bad. I close my locker and turn to respond to her, but as I do, my eyes land on Marco in the distance.

As soon as the scene registers in my mind, I feel the bile crawling up my esophagus and pooling in my mouth.

Only thirty yards down the hallway, there he stood, but he's not alone. He had a life-size fake-tanned Barbie pressed up against the lockers by the hips, and his hands were gripping her cutoff jean skirt at the waist. I feel the tears building in my eyes like nimbostratus clouds expanding, shrinking the blue sky into nothing as he gently brushes a lock of her bleach-blond hair behind her triple-pierced ear. I want to turn away to save face, but I'm too paralyzed to move.

I see Mrs. Taylor put two and two together. "Oh, Honey." She places her hands on my shoulders and turns me to face her. "Some boys would rather search for greener pastures than water their own grass. Don't you dare let that boy get to you. One day, a man will step up, and you won't even think about that boy you dated in high school that couldn't see your worth."

I don't even try to stop the tears from falling down, and Mrs. Taylor brushes them away with her thumb as she cradles my chin in her tiny hand. I want to say something—anything—to move past this awkward embrace, but I know it is one of those times that if I move, I'll lose it. Like "ugly cry, run from the building, pack my bags, move to Mississippi, and live on a goddamn farm" lose it.

The bell rings, everyone files into their prospective classrooms, and the hallways clear out quickly. I watch Marco slowly strut away, the life-size Barbie flanking his right, and he turns around once more to make sure his exit is noted. With a smirk, he puts his arm around the blond, and she answers by toying with his fingers that were laced in mine only two days ago. I can still feel the ache of its absence.

I turn to Mrs. Taylor and ask, "May I please go to the bathroom?"

"Sure, hun. Just come back when you feel up to it. We are finishing *The Scarlet Letter* today! I could really use your insight to get the conversation going!"

"Yes, ma'am," and she leaves me in the empty hallway as she closes the door behind her.

As I make my way to the nearest toilet, I see Marco walking toward me with his hands in his pockets. I slow down, and we are now facing each other with only two feet of space between us.

"You gonna go puke?"

"Where's Barbie?"

"I put her away. We'll play later."

"Why are you such an *ass*?"

"Why are you such a *freak*?"

"*Freak*? You're calling me a freak?"

"If the shoe fits—"

"I wish I never met you."

"Well, find a lamp, Rube, and rub it. Let me know how it goes."

"I thought you loved me, Marco."

"No one's ever gonna love you, Ruby. You won't *let* them."

"How can you be *so* mean?"

"How can you be so *blind*?"

"What the hell is that supposed to mean?"

"It means you're killing yourself. I just can't sit back and watch it."

"So you run to *her*?"

"Her parents have a house on the lake. She invited me to Vail with them in December. I'm going, Rube. I've got to move on from this toxic back-and-forth with you. It's getting ridiculous."

"It's only back-and-forth because you can't keep your eyes on me. You're always looking for someone better."

"That's because I've outgrown you, Ruby. Don't you get it? You're not on my level anymore. You're wasting away to nothing, and all you care about is what goes in your mouth and how to get rid of it."

"Because that's what you taught me, Marco! I'm only doing what you taught me!"

"You're delusional. Leave me alone. I'm done with you, Rube, for real."

"Marco—"

"I mean it, Ruby. I'm *done*." He walked past me, brushing my shoulder with his as he passed, as if I'm a stranger only 2.5 seconds after he's said his peace. As he turns left at the end of the hallway, he places his hand on the corner of the wall and lets his body disappear completely before his hand lingers like a fingerprint left on a mirror that distracts you from seeing anything but a greasy streak left for all to see. Marco is my greasy streak. Little did I know how hard it would be to remove that stain from my soul.

"Ruby, where are you going?" Mrs. Taylor called after me, realizing I was heading down the hallway. I didn't answer, and she didn't follow me.

I followed the wolf out the double doors and walked into the morning sun with every intention to appease my anxious heart, and not even my favorite teacher Mrs. Taylor can stop me. My house is only a mile down the road, and the pantry and bathroom will be unsupervised for hours.

Glad they only eat to live because I'm about to do some do some damage to the pantry.

CHAPTER 6

Tuesday, October 19, 2021

The afternoon sun blares through the passenger side window, and I shift my knees to lean up against the door. The heat that's accompanying the rays is brutal, but I prefer it to Michael at the moment. Car rides during a fight are how I'd prefer to interact. It's a forced face-forward situation, and I'm thankful I don't have to look at him. I stare blankly at the passing trees that are starting to turn the slightest sunset orange in the afternoon sun. I suddenly feel the emotion rising in my throat, and I swallow hard and look up to the sky. I once heard that if you look up, you are less likely to cry. It seems to work, and I focus on the clouds moving slowly in the autumn breeze.

I told a coworker about Michael's mistake today, and the reaction I got was not what I expected. She said, "Oh, Ruby, that's it? That's all he did? That's nothing. It happens in our friend group all the time. A little flirting and fantasizing keeps things interesting." Goes to show that not everyone has the same standards in marriage, and what works for some may not work for others. My self-confidence is still fragile, so I'm okay with disagreeing with her. I'm *not* okay with flirting in my marriage, probably because of my experiences with it in my past relationships.

Flirting opens doors that could easily remain shut otherwise.

I've worked too hard to build the life I want for meaningless flirtation to ruin it all, and I'm *still* in shock that Michael was so careless.

Recently, we purchased our dream property in Western North Carolina. We've lived below our means for so long, and now it's *finally* paying off. It's on the corner of Sweetleaf and Wineberry, and we lovingly refer to it as *Sweetleaf.* It seems unreal to finally have the perfect three acres with a waterfall on site nestled in the heart of Round Mountain. As soon as we stepped foot on it and felt the peace it brought us, we knew we had to make the bold move to buy it on the spot. Michael and I had a very modest yet sweet beginning, and thinking about it makes my heart smile even through the uncertainty of our current situation.

We were so, so young.

*****

In 2007, I was a first-year teacher, fresh out of college, and newly single. I stayed in the small town that I did my student teaching in because after Weston and I called it quits, I felt lost. Once again, I was literally scared to move, afraid I would spiral even more out of control with my ED in overdrive. Although I knew I didn't want to be in Mississippi, I was scared to move away on my own again, and there was no way I could face my family when I was that disordered. I needed time to make a life plan, so staying comfortably miserable beat out taking a leap of faith to risk happiness. It's really a messed up way of living, if you think about it.

New Hope, Mississippi is a two-stoplight town with the main food option at the time being the gas station that sold fried chicken that I refused to eat. My students couldn't fathom the fact that I was twenty-three years old and single, so they set out on a mission to hook me up with the only other single outsider in the whole town.

"Ms. Brooks, you've got to meet Coach Blue!" My sweet tenth grader Tarren sang as she and her best friend Roxanne plopped themselves on the desks closest to mine after the final bell rang. I was attempting to grade papers, but there was always a steady stream of students who needed attention, so my attempts were usually pointless.

"Who's Coach Blue?" I asked with a skeptical eye.

"Oh, he's the assistant varsity boys basketball coach!" Roxanne offered as if I'd be impressed. Basketball was big in New Hope. They were in the running for the state championship this season, but I couldn't care less.

I hate basketball.

"Ugh. Basketball? I don't know about that. I'm more of a baseball kind of girl," I joke, trying to politely duck out of this conversation, but my curiosity gets the best of me. "How old is he?"

"Twenty, I think," Tarren offers. "He is a junior in college, but he is in school to be a teacher, so he coaches for extra money. He drives my bus sometimes too. He lives with his parents next to my friend. I think he's from Pennsylvania?"

Twenty?
Basketball coach?
College student?
Bus driver?
Lives with parents?

83

Hell no.

"Well, as lovely as he sounds, I think I'm good. He seems a bit…young for me." Almost three years, to be exact. He's a baby. He's got two more years of college, *and* he's a coach. I already learned years ago that I couldn't date a hunter. Gone every weekend to stalk, kill, and eat innocent animals—no, thank you. I have friends who have dated coaches before, and they say it's brutally similar. Although I love sports, I don't want to be stuck in a smelly high school gym supporting my man when I could be *anywhere* else. "Is he cute?"

"Um…kind of, in a way," Tarren hesitates. "I mean, he has potential!"

Potential?

Yikes.

"Well, I guess if he is interested in meeting me, he can come down to my room," I half-heartedly suggest as I go back to the papers on my desk.

"Cool. We'll go get him." And before I even had the chance to protest, the two cheerleaders were racing out of my room, book bags flying behind them.

Shit! That escalated quickly.

Not five minutes later, I hear a quiet *knock, knock*, and my heart jumps in my throat as I see him leaning on the doorframe. He is tall, slim built, but I can tell that under his shirt lies that lean type of muscle that makes my hands ache with anticipation. He has green eyes that are slightly angled puppy-dog style, and his strong nose and chin make my knees go a little weak. I put down the papers I was holding, and I wipe my hands on my slacks and trip on my computer cord as I round the desk to make myself more available.

Damn, kind of cute?

This dude is more than cute.

"Hey, Ms. Brooks, I'm Michael. The kids call me Blue. I thought I'd stop by and introduce myself. I heard you are new to this town. It's tiny, and outsiders like you and me have to stick together." He winks, and I'm done.

I collect myself and offer my hand. "Hello! Call me Ruby. It still feels so weird to be called Ms. Brooks."

He reaches out to shake my hand, and his grip is firm, strong. He has big hands. My feet start to sweat.

"All right then, Ruby. It is nice to meet you." He shyly smiled and slowly released his grip on my hand. I wished he had held it longer.

"For sure!" I added, and then it happened. What always happens when I'm nervous: I began to ramble. A "babbling Brooks" is what I turn into, and it is so embarrassing.

I don't even know what I said, but I think I told him my life story in one breath and at double the speed of a normal conversation. All I remember is that he stood there, leaning in, smiling as I went on and on, and when he got a chance to get a word in, he made his move.

"I have to run back to practice, but can we continue this get-to-know-you session outside of work sometime?"

Um, hell yes!

Can shirts be optional?

"I would love that."

"Great. Want to go to the pep rally with me Friday night? I know a great barbecue place outside of town that has the best pulled pork around. Nothing like they have up north. And you Southerners sure do know how to make sweet tea!" He patted his stomach, but all I could think about was his hands.

I hate barbecue, and I despise sweet tea. I've been told more than once that my Southern card should be revoked. I actually hate eating in general, so I'm no stranger to faking it when it comes to meals. I have my ways to "get rid" of it, but that is not appropriate first-time-meeting talk, and even I can control my tongue in this case.

"That sounds great! I'm looking forward to it."

"Okay, Ruby. I'll see you Friday." He smiles and turns to walk out the door. As he is about to leave, he adds, "And remind me to thank your girls Tarren and Roxanne. They did me a solid today!"

"Don't thank them too much. They said you weren't that cute," I tease, and he takes the bait.

"Well, you said yes to Friday, so I will take that as you're a woman that thinks for herself." And with that, he disappeared into the hallway and left me to melt.

*****

The silence in the space between us allows the disorder to whisper sweet nothings to my vulnerable, thirsty soul, and I shake my head to clear the toxic demands. It's times like these that my ED sneaks in to attempt to regain control. Today, my brain is focusing on the fact that Michael wanted someone else enough to actually *act* on it. I feel so stupid for being blindsided. I should have seen this coming, but how could I? He's got a lot of areas he can improve, as we all do, but loyalty has never been one of them.

I wish I was in the woods.

"Where are we going?" The road we're on was taking us away from home, so my curiosity forced me to break the silence between us, and I noticed his hands on the wheel— still big, still strong, still gives me chills to think about them.

"To Mulberry Park," he states without shifting his eyes off the road. "I know you love the trails there, so I figured we could take a hike, if you're up for it. The kids are with friends, so we're free to do whatever, but I know you've been missing the woods." I hate him for knowing me so well. Anytime I'm upset, I crave to be under the trees. When I'm under the protective umbrella of their leaves, it makes me feel safe. There's a thick, calm energy that gets trapped between the earth and their branches that feels like a gift every time I breathe in. My favorite book when I was little was *The Giving Tree* by Shel Silverstein, and the theme of love and selflessness that the tree saturates the boy with truly gave me comfort and hope for a love like that one day.

A good friend once described our connections with others in relation to trees. And over the years, the comparison has stuck with me. Faith is the root of our tree. It gives us life, stability, and connection to this world and those around us. Our soul mate in this life is our trunk. It's the base and the life of the tree, present for life's biggest moments, and helping to guide and shape our existence through the years. Our chosen family are our branches. The people who create the beauty, heart, and wonder of our world as we reach out and toward the sky. And then there are people in our lives who are our leaves. These are fleeting relationships that come and go with the seasons of life, and although they are beautiful while they last, they disappear and wither away inevitably with time.

Michael has been my trunk for fifteen years, but today, I feel like the stump at the end of Silverstein's story—used, underappreciated, and only recognized as the gift I once was.

"Sure," is all I give him. I notice the book *The Four Agreements* tucked under his console, and I wonder why he has it. The other week, I tried to read him the parable at the beginning about all living things being made of the same material as the stars, but he was snoring in minutes. I sneak a look across the cab, and a pang of longing tingles up my spine. I've always told him that he's ruggedly handsome, and time's been good to him. He gets more and more sexy every year, and I hate him for it at this moment.

As we pull into the parking lot, I get out of the car quickly so that Michael doesn't get a chance to open my door. I know the trails of the park from my ultra-marathoning days, and I head right for the creek trailhead.

I need moving water.

I hear the stream before I see it. Its sound washes over me like a deep breath, and I can feel the air temperature dropping the closer and closer we get to the bank. There is a spot where it's clear enough to sit, but there's just enough coverage so that other patrons of the park will not disturb your peace. When I'm in the woods, I prefer to be alone. As the clearing emerges, I can smell the sweetness of the sourwood trees that thrive in this environment.

Me too, sourwood.

I don't even pay attention to the dampness of the ground. I plop down and immediately put my Chacos in the water to let the freezing current wash away my anxiety. Michael cautiously sits down a good six feet to my left and places the book between us. That is one thing I can't stand about him. Even after being together for fifteen years, he still can't put his feelings aside to just hold me when I need it. If he'd just hold me, I could feel safe again. I could understand that he's sorry and that he didn't mean what he said to Camryn. But alas, there he sits, six feet away, and the torment of the space between us is overwhelming.

I reach for the book and open it to the parable to focus my thoughts. I can sense Michael watching me read, and I give him a side-eye as a warning. He grins and turns back toward the stream. "I skipped work today. I read that instead." He nods to Ruiz's treasure in my lap. "You know, the one you asked your asshole husband to read with you, and then he fell asleep?"

You said it, not me.

"What'd ya think?" And I go on pretending to read.

"I think I should've read that book a long time ago, and maybe we wouldn't be sitting here."

Chills run up my spine. I've felt this regret before. I divert my eyes up to the sky to be safe. The wolves start pacing in my mind, and I begin to pick at my nonexistent nails. I've destroyed them since Saturday, but I could be coping in worse ways. I've barely eaten, but at least I haven't thrown up. I've been behavior free since June of this year. The pandemic had me slipping back into some old temptations, but I checked back in with Dr. Sapphire to keep me on track. I'll do *anything* not to fall back down the dark wormhole of my eating disorder. A repeat of 2016 ain't an option.

I can't relapse.

"To really answer your question, as I was reading it, I felt more and more peace with every word. The shame and guilt I've been choking on for so long started to surface, and it's like I was finally able to spit it out. Each agreement feels like it was written for me."

"Some think that it's saturated in conventional morality," I challenge, and he bites.

"Rubes, not all of us share your extensive knowledge of human psychology, so if you could translate, that would help."

"We paid enough for treatment, so at least you know I learned something from my time at Manna House! And actually, I learned this at State. It's Kohlberg's theory on moral development. I'll spare you the details, but it basically defines humans' level of morality based on their willingness to conform. Preconventional, conventional, and postconventional are the three stages. The conventional stage will accept the majority's perception of right and wrong, basically following the crowd, the opposite of free thinking."

"I don't know about all that, but I feel like it did the opposite for me."

"How?" I'm interested. He's actually read this book, and I'm curious to where this is going.

"Well, it made me take a look at my shortcomings through a different lens. Reading those agreements made me realize how often I break my own morals and try to brush the evidence under the rug, and when my shit's exposed, I blame anyone or anything but me." He wipes his nose with the back of his knuckles. "It told me I'm gonna screw up because I'm human, but also, here are the ways I can minimize that. If you wanna call me a sheep, so be it. At least I'll be able to sleep soundly at night knowing I've done my best today."

"See why you should've read it before Saturday?" I couldn't resist the jab, but he takes it square.

"Absolutely." He nods with his lips pursed, and for once, I know the anger is not toward me. "I can't believe how stupid I was, but instead of dwell on it, I want to take action."

"Like the action you proposed to Camryn?"

"Camryn didn't deserve any of that, and I will apologize to her when she's ready to allow me the honor, but for now, I have to work on myself. That's what the agreements taught me." He shifts the conversation to focus on me. "What makes you love this book so much? It's been a while since I have seen you this passionate about teaching a novel. The last time you were this vocal with me about a book was when they took *To Kill a Mockingbird* from your curriculum."

I think about where to start. How do I explain to him the impact that this book has had on me the past few weeks? Ironically, my mom suggested it to me as a segue into *The Alchemist* for my ninth graders, and after I heard her describe its message, I went to the bookstore and bought it immediately. I rushed home, sat down, and read it in three hours.

How do I describe something that gave mapped out directions to my mission of self-love and self-acceptance?

"It gave me permission to exist in the moment without expecting perfection from myself or others, and I would not be able to forgive myself if I didn't share it with my students."

Everyone has their own wolves.

"Your students are really lucky to have you. These are really tangible tools that can actually help them work through their problems. Hell, everyone has to start somewhere, and it's hard without a guide." He stared into my eyes as he turned his hat backward and scooted closer to me. Both of our energies have shifted since we sat by the water, and I'm reminded that our core peace is obtained so similarly in nature. I'm feeling more open, and his smile was warm and promising.

And when he turns that hat backwards...

"You've been really quiet since I messed up, so I'm actually terrified of what's been going on in your brain, Rubes." I don't respond. "But you're still here with me, so I'm counting that as a win." He reaches out and tucks a stray hair behind my ear. I lean in just enough to give him hope, but then recoil in fear. "I know I've got so much to prove to you, Rubes. I do. I can't say it anymore. I just have to do it."

I want to forgive him. I want to fall in his arms. But how can I trust that I'm enough?

My mind flashes back to the morning my parents told Charleigh and me that they were getting a divorce. I remember the fear, confusion, and hurt like it was yesterday. Nali's around the same age as I was when Dad moved out, and I shudder even thinking about having that conversation with my two kids. Hudson wouldn't be okay. I put my face in my hands and rubbed my eyes.

We have to make this work.
We can't do that to the kids.
I refuse.

"Divorce isn't an option for me."

"Thank you, Jesus," Michael prayed into his palms with a whimper.

"I love Jesus and all, but my view on divorce has zero to do with the Bible and everything to do with our two children." My voice cracked. I look at him, and I see his chin shaking.

"You have no idea how much this means to me to hear you say that, Rubes. You, Nali, and Hud are my world, and I never want to put our family in jeopardy again." He turns to face the stream and wipes a tear off of his cheek. He doesn't cry often. On our wedding day, when I walked down the aisle, he lost it. He cried the entire ceremony, and everyone said it was the sweetest groom moment they'd ever seen. He still claims there were gnats in his eyes. "Honestly, I think my proposition to Camryn was a dumb cry for help. As messed up as it sounds, I knew that she'd say no. That was obvious. And then I knew she'd tell you. Somehow, subconsciously, I think I needed to be kicked out so I'd be forced to face my feelings."

"What feelings, Michael? I'm so confused. We've come *so* damn far. Do you not want this? Do you not want me?" I plead.

"I haven't had a chance to process you almost *dying*, Ruby. Until recently, you've needed me to be strong. I had to be the rock. I've stood by you, Rubes, through the eating disorder, the running addiction, the attempts to figure out who you truly are, and I'm so damn proud of you and what you've accomplished for you, our kids, our marriage. But *I've* never been able to break. I've never had the chance to falter. And now that you're healed, I saw how much you thrived having Camryn around, and I was hurt. I wanted you to have that joy and ease with me, but you didn't. Sometimes it feels as if she's the missing piece for you." His eyes were fixed on the water, and mine could've burned a hole through his skull.

"So your solution is to invite her to our bedroom? Great plan, Michael. Ten out of ten." My response is dismissive, and I feel bad about brushing over his confession, but I just can't get past my hurt yet.

"I'm an idiot, Rubes. No, I'm a coward. I should've talked to you about what I was feeling." His voice was high-pitched and saturated with sobs. "I know, and I'm sorry. Instead of talking to you, I got drunk and jacked everything up. I love you so damn much, Rubes. I know I have messed up, but I promise I'll do whatever it takes to make this right. I just need you by my side to get through it."

I've never questioned Michael's love for me. He's right. It took all hands on deck for me to survive my anxiety, eating disorder, and running addiction. We've survived *my* break-down. Maybe it's his turn to fall apart.

I slip my hand across the damp earth and close the gap between us. I slid my fingers lightly across his. He shifted his weight to free up his arms, and he wrapped one around my waist and pulled me into his embrace. I let my body melt into his, and my head found its way to his chest.

Suddenly, I'm seven years old, back in the Watsons Place house, watching two people in a lightning storm deep in love and sadness share a life-changing moment, except this time, the outcome will be different.

He's always fought for me.
It is now my turn to fight for him.

CHAPTER 7

Saturday, August 16, 2003

To say I procrastinated on making a decision where I'd go to college after Clemson fell through would be an understatement. I waited until the last second, and then I threw a Hail Mary out to every college in the Southeastern Conference and swore I'd pick the first one that accepted me. Mississippi State got back to me in under two weeks, so I packed my car and headed west on I-20 to a state I'd never even been to before.

I'm now sitting in my bedroom alone, thoughts spiraling as usual. I don't like how big this soapbox house is. It's quiet and empty. It has four bedrooms, five baths, and it is surprisingly reasonable to rent for its size.

Welcome to Mississippi.

The neighborhood is new construction, paper-thin houses for college kids that line State's golf course. Dorms were my first choice, but since I was a late admission, they were all full by the time I registered. I look around at the white cube I'm now living in, and all I can think is, *there's no way this could hold up to a tornado.* The ceilings are at least twelve feet high, and the space feels foreign to the point of eerie. The walls are stark white and bare. It reminds me of an awkward empty yoga studio. Every time I move an item, I hear the echo bounce off the four bare walls with vigor. The ceiling fan makes an obnoxious clicking sound, and it's too high for me to adjust it.

Tink, tink, tink, tink.

I contemplate throwing a pillow at it but decide the *tink* is better than the damn thing falling on my head, so I refrain. I scoot the full-size bed to the corner under the window so I can at least see *some* nature, but the view just makes me even more depressed. I look out over the sunburned fairway with miles and miles of flat farmland stretching out to the horizon behind it. My stomach flips, and I swallow back the growing self-doubt.

I should've visited before just packing the entirety of my life and moving here.

The flatland mocks my impulsivity, and I can imagine the "I told you so" that would proudly come out of their mouths if I were to call them to admit I made a mistake coming here. I miss the mountains. I miss the hills. I miss the trees. The trees here are young, one-per-yard Bradford pears that are planted poorly and falling over. I bet you can see a storm coming for miles, though, like when you're standing on the edge of the ocean at the beach, and you can see the clouds building and building in the distance, and you know right when it's gonna hit. I can almost imagine seeing them roll in off the cotton fields as I try to find anything positive to grasp onto.

I love storms.

I had to be potluck placed with random roommates because I don't know a soul here in Starkville, but I and one girl from Northern Mississippi must've been the last two desperate loners standing because they put us in that huge house alone. Her name's Joanna (*said in a deep, proud Miss'ippi accent*), and she's barely come out of her room since we moved in. I had high hopes to have the meet-your-soul-sister college experience, but I'm thinking I may have to get a cat to fulfill that role judging by my first interactions with the reclusive stranger upstairs.

Wolves don't like cats.

Although the people here are superfriendly, Mississippi's a tight-knit state. Outsiders are treated kindly, but accepted is a different monster. Take my new neighbors for example. They are from Itta Bena, Mississippi, which they proudly refer to as *the Delta*. They invited me over for a cookout yesterday since it was my first night in the neighborhood, and I already made an ass of myself. I asked the cook to pass me the ketchup. He pounded his fists on the table and said, "*Yankee, we don't use no ketchup on our steaks down here in Miss'ippi. You can kindly leave if that's how you 'tend on eatin' my meat.*" I thought about backpedaling and making a joke about "*eatin' his meat,*" but when no one else was smiling, I decided to just shut up. I learned quickly to hide any non-Mississippi traits that I embodied.

When in Rome...

There's a long list of things that I learned just from freshman orientation: Abercrombie & Fitch isn't cool, camouflage is a key part of one's wardrobe, monograms go on *everything*, you can only shop at boutiques, and not drinking beer or sweet tea is an *actual* sin. Also, I'm a freak for never eating crawfish, I'm a wuss for not liking spicy food, and I need to put "meat on my bones" has been said to me no less than twenty-two times. I've never lived anywhere other than the suburbs outside of Atlanta, so the culture shock's a level ten, for sure. But in true Ruby fashion, I'd rather suffer in silence than admit to my family that they may have been right after all. I could be living it up in Athens with Charleigh and Robert right now, but Marco's there too.

I'll take being an outsider in Mississippi over a pawn in his reckless game of chess any day.

It's late, and my stomach is growling (which isn't abnormal since I only feed it once a day), and I step cautiously out of my room that's directly off the kitchen. I immediately see Joanna sitting at the counter, pushing scrambled eggs around her plate. I give her a smile and say the cheesiest line: "Great minds think alike!" and the regret is immediate. She keeps her face turned toward her eggs and cuts a side-eye to meet mine in disapproval. She has beautiful brown eyes, big teased brown locks that fall right below her shoulders, and she sits with her legs crossed like she is at a fancy restaurant even though she's merely sitting solo at our empty kitchen island in her sweats.

"Well, I fig'erd that I best eat before my stomach ate my backbone." She almost spit the phrase at me with no smile on her face. Her Northern Mississippi accent is the thickest I've ever experienced, and I'm not sure how I'm gonna understand her. She took a deep breath as if to gather the patience to speak to me. "You're from At'lana, right? How much you like gradua'tin?"

I stared at her in confusion, my eyes searching her face for any sign of what she'd just asked me with no luck. I grabbed the tuna from the cabinet and said, "Yes, outside of Atlanta, but what was that last part of your question?"

She rolled her eyes and repeated, "I said, 'How much you like gradua'tin?'" She took a bite of eggs, and her stare only got more impatient.

What the hell is she asking me? If I *like* graduation? Is she serious? "Joanna, I really don't know yet if I like graduating. I'm not done with school yet."

"Dangit, Ruby, *how much school you got left until you grad'uate?*"

"Oh, lack! I thought you were saying *like!* I was so confused!" I laughed that awkward laugh that's forced out to fill the silence but cut it short. "I'm sorry. I haven't gotten used to the accents here yet. I'm a freshman, so I'll be here for at least four years. I'm an English major, but I think I want to teach!"

"If ya cain't under'stan English, then how ya gonna teach it! Lord help them kids." She finished off her eggs and put her fork on her plate with a clang and whipped the corners of her mouth.

I tried to change the subject. "So is '*my stomach is eating my backbone*' a Mississippi saying? That one's new to me!"

"I don't know. My did'y always says it." She politely got up to clean her plate.

"Your what?" I asked before I thought about how me questioning her accent on day one may not be a good thing.

"My did'y. Ya know? My dad? What the hell do you call your did'ys in Georgia, by their government names?" She washed and dried it with a rag and then put it back up in the cabinet. I can tell she's clean, and I'm happy about that.

"My bad." I don't even know how to have a conversation without offending this girl, so this living arrangement should be fun. I open the can of tuna and dig my fork in. I take a big bite and the juice runs down my chin. I wipe it with my sleeve, and I can feel Joanna's stare.

"Are you really eatin' raw tuna from a can? 'Mind me to never go home with you for Thanksgivin'," and she disappeared up the stairs to her room. I think she likes having the whole upstairs to herself. At least she can avoid explaining every other word or phrase to me.

Maybe there's something to the saying there's no place like home.

It took a Mississippi minute for Joanna to warm up to me. Although we shared very similar backgrounds struggling with our mental health, we definitely coped with them differently. She was "*blinds closed*," and I was "*blinds open*." I was "*let's go drink*," and she was "*let's turn on a Reba and nap*." I was "*put on a crop top and get your ass out the door*," and she was "*let's make brownies and listen to the country music countdown*." But somehow, we each became the best friend neither of us wanted to admit we needed.

My transition into Mississippi can be compared to moving to a country where I don't speak the language. The dialect, the traditions, the beliefs—it's all so different from where I grew up, and I got low-key depressed the first six months in Starkville. My fantasy of moving away and "showing them all" was dead on arrival. I missed my family, I missed my familiar town, and I missed the comfort of fitting in. The farms for miles and miles are beautiful, but the landscape doesn't fill my soul the same way the mountains and woods do. It's hard to live in a place that I don't love geographically when that's where I get most of my peace.

I wish I was under the trees.

If I'm honest, my move to Mississippi was my way of avoiding anyone who cares about me enough to hold me accountable for my actions. Not only do I not know anyone here, I also have my own room and bathroom for the first time ever, so there's no one there to watch/regulate my every move. I'm alone for the first time in my life, and I've figured out I have no idea who I am or what I like.

I do like throwing up.

I didn't know how addictive puking could actually be. When my stomach is full, I imagine all the heaviness of my past swirling in the depths of my gut, and this time, I have control of the chaos' destination. I can conjure up all my hurt, all my pain, all my disappointment, and force it out all at once like a bullet from a gun. Once the trigger is pulled, the target will be met, and it won't take but a second to drop it dead. To me, the release is euphoric; like the time that's both lost and gained in a deep sleep. Hell, I'd even prefer it over an orgasm; that's how freakin' good it feels. I know how disgusting it may seem to someone who's never experienced it, but it feels like the first thing that I have in my life that's mine and no one can take it away.

Except the wolves love to see my bones.

Sounds ridiculous, huh? I know it is, but I *still* stick my fingers down my throat and get rid of food to feel relief. Every time I purge, it's a therapy session without the overwhelming task of digging through all the emotional trauma that I'd rather burn than let it burn me.

Having my own place is fantastic for my eating disorder, but I can tell it's already taking a toll on my body. I have developed really bad acid reflux, and anytime I actually keep food down, my stomach freaks out and causes my bowels to dump everything in my entire existence. As a result, I'm thin as hell with blown-up cheeks, and I'm constantly having dizzy spells.

I passed out from puking just last week. I came home from class one afternoon, ate a bowl of popcorn, and didn't drink enough water to bring it back up, and I choked on the dry, gravel-like remains of the kernels that were adamant on mucking up my plans. Panic set in when I was trying to clear my airway. I desperately attempted to clear the lodged hash from the back of my throat with my fingers, but all that did was poke dents in the mush like putty. The bathroom began spinning from under my knees, and I must have lost consciousness because when I woke up, I was lying on the tile floor in a pool of my own vomit.

Yeah, not good.

After that experience, I vowed to give up purging by puking. It was becoming too dangerous. Unfortunately, now, instead of throwing up, I rarely eat and run off anything that I actually do. The golf course barely gets used, so I can run the cart paths all day long and not bother anyone. The release of sweat and energy from my pores is like a prolonged puke, so I get a similar satisfaction. Plus, it's socially acceptable and keeps my stomach flat, so it's a win-win. I started out just running a mile a day, but I'm now up to six, and I'm getting pretty fast.

Perk of the disorder, I guess.

Running has given me purpose in a place where I feel lost. My ED has become my spirit guide pointing in the direction I shall go, and it knows I will comply every time. The road is my savior, and the pounding of my feet is my hymnal. Here in the Bible Belt of the South, my church is getting lost on the back roads that carry me far away from myself. I'm free when I'm in motion. It's only when I'm still that the wolves can find me.

I've learned that Joanna doesn't share my love for running. She's a smoker, and her hair's way too amazing to subject it to sweat and a ponytail. One day, she was taking a nap after class, and I burst through her door in full workout gear. I went straight to the blinds, as I always do, and I yanked the cord with a vengeance so that the screeching of the thin metal would shake her from her slumber. She, as she always does, pulled the comforter over her face and created her cocoon of darkness, but I didn't stop there. I jumped on her bed and shook her into existence.

"Wake up, sleepyhead! I need some company on my run. Hop to it!" I wrestled with her for control of the covers, and she finally gave up, knowing that I would not stop until she acknowledged me.

"Dangit, Ruby, I ain't go'en on no run! The only way I'm run'in is'f som'then is chasin' me."

"Come on. Don't make me go on my own! It's a beautiful day! We can even walk. Come on, plllleeeeeasssssseeeee!" I wrap her in a bear hug where I'm the big spoon, and she giggles, and then remembers herself.

"Git off me! You're crazy. Fine. If it'll make you leave me the hell alone, I'll go." She groans and takes off her fuzzy socks and replaces them with her Nike ones that are barely broken in. I jump off her bed and dart down the stairs like a dog that finally sees its owner reaching for the leash. I know how rare it is for her to accept an invitation to work out, so I'm not giving her a chance to back out!

She trudged down the steps at a snail's pace, and she rolled her eyes at me as I stood by the open front door like a kid who just was told to *get in the car, we are going out for ice cream!*

"I still don't git it. How the hell can you think that runnin' is fun? Makes no sense." She stepped into the Mississippi sunlight and deliberately placed her Ray-Bans on to shield her eyes.

"It's good for you to get out of that room for something other than class. By the way, I'm impressed that you have been making class a priority lately! What's with the change?" I questioned.

"Mama said if my grades drop anymore, she's gonna come down here and drag my ass home, and I ain't doin' it. My damn brother and his girlfriend are livin' at the house now, and I cain't stand be'in 'round her ass. She's trash." She pulls out a menthol cigarette and puts it between her lips. Her left hand shields the stick as she sparks the lighter, and she turns to me with her hand on her hip. "Well, we goin' or not?" A stream of smoke billows from her rounded lips.

I just shake my head. "Really, Joanna? You're smoking while we exercise?" I flash her one of her own famous eye rolls, and she dismisses the gesture with a flip of her hand and takes a big drag. She's unapologetically herself, and it truly gives me hope that one day, I can find myself too. I'm seeing more and more of my personality blossom since getting away from my hometown, and it feels more freeing than depressing these days.

We begin our power walk down the street, and a jeep containing two frat boys speeds past us with its windows and doors off. The driver yells, "Smoke that cigarette, baby!" and his and the passenger's laugh is louder than the Linkin Park banger blasting on the speakers.

"Take a picture. It lasts longer!" She took a puff and blew the smoke over her right shoulder in the jeep's direction. I laugh so hard, I almost pee my pants, and I'm reminded once again how lucky I am that the universe put us together. She may be my complete opposite, but she completes me perfectly.

That was the only time Joanna exercised with me because my running routine became increasingly intense. My regimen was set in stone, and rain, shine, or sickness, I completed it daily. I woke up at 6:00 a.m. before the sun became unbearable, and I would run an hour on the golf course before class. The mornings were my processing time of the day. Since Joanna was really my only friend, the drama that I experienced in high school was nonexistent now in college. I liked being out of the fray, but it does get lonely. Although Joanna is a great friend, she can't satisfy my physical wants and needs.

There are some fine country boys here in Mississippi. Not gonna lie.

After class, I would hit the gym for weights and swimming. MSU is the only school in the SEC that does not have a swim and dive team, so I can swim laps with the old men in Speedos without getting triggered. My first meal of the day is usually around 4:00 p.m., and it consists of a two-ounce can of tuna mixed with about two tablespoons of baked beans for flavor. Then I go on a night run around 9:30 p.m. on the main street leading to downtown, and it allows me to safely observe all the normal college students having fun and enjoying life. I watch them with envy as they laugh and drink on the patio porches and high rooftop bars. The girls are dressed to the nines, and the guys wear collared shirts and khakis. Sperrys are abundant, and hair flips go with every conversation regardless of what gender they are. It makes me feel really out of place in my sweaty tank top and Nikes. I have never been one to be shy, but Mississippi's like a foreign land to me, and that makes meeting people more intimidating than it's ever been. When I'm done with my night run, I shower, drink my thirty-two-ounce water bottle, and go to bed with Food Network on quietly in the background. I know I should eat more, but I'm not throwing up anymore, so I'm calling that a win.

As for my dating life, I figured out early that the Delta boys, although hot, are not my type. It took me going to a guy's hunting camp one time to determine that. I killed a deer then laid on it and cried for forty-five minutes *and then* was forced to try chitlins. I should've known after he yelled about ketchup, but I always like to learn the hard way. I also jumped around the sorority and fraternity scene for a bit, but I was thankful I didn't buy into that phony hype like I did in fifth grade when they coerced me into a middle school band. I can still taste that rotten reed. Although they were gentlemen to the bone, these State studs were a bit too drenched in fresh animal blood for my liking.

However, there was a group of people that I didn't even know existed: the Mississippi hippies. They were literally the perfect fit for me, minus the marijuana.

Weed makes me feel like my teeth are touching.

They travel to watch live music every weekend, and bands like Yonder Mountain and Dave Matthews were favorites, but really, anywhere there's a guitar and a soulful voice, the Mississippi hippies were there! Bonus! They're into extreme outdoor activities that I grew to *love*. Hiking, mountain biking, kayaking, and camping were always a part of the plan. Every day is an opportunity for a new adventure, and I was thankful to be along for the ride!

*****

It was a balmy fall day when I met the two boys who would change the trajectory of my Mississippi experience. I was on a run down through the Cotton District, and when I got to the busy intersection at the bank, I stopped to avoid getting hit. Just as I stopped, I spotted a little gray kitten huddled in the safety of the storm drain ahead. I darted across the intersection that was clear seconds ago, and that's when I heard the sound of tires screeching. I had no time to look, just react, so I dove across the street and landed in a heap on the opposite sidewalk. My knees and elbows burned, and I slowly lifted myself up off the concrete.

"Are you okay?" I heard a voice ask, but I was not able to focus on his face. I reached for my knees to examine the damage. My elbows were bleeding pretty well, but the scrapes on my knees gave me flashbacks of epic rollerblade crashes that left me raw and embarrassed.

"I think so." I looked up to meet the stranger's gaze. He was tall, about six feet two inches, had chocolate curly hair, and an Adam's apple that I yearned to see bounce up and down his throat again, and looked older than me by a few years. He sat down next to me and explained the scene.

"Man, I was standing in line at the ATM, and I heard the tires. I looked over, and I saw you flying. I thought you were hit, but it looks like you just superwomaned yourself out of the way, so I'm actually thankful to just see your knees and 'bows scraped. I can do blood. I can't do splattered brains!" He has a big toothy grin that looks like it would taste like Cherry Coke.

He's really handsome.

"No, they didn't hit me, but it was close! I was trying to get that cat over there. He better be grateful!" I say as I attempt to fix my ponytail. I'm sure I look *amazing* after a run and almost dying in the process.

He laughs and heads toward the kitten. "You mean this little guy?" He comes back, and he is cupping the kitten with one hand. It is a tiny ball of gray and white fur, and he is thankful for the friendly hand that is caressing him.

Okay, hot guy and a kitten—way too predictable. Is this a joke?

He passes the little guy to me, and I know instantly he'll have to be ripped from my dead hands. "Can I walk you home?" The guy I almost forgot about politely asks, and I agree. As we walk, we get a lotta funny looks. Here is this sweaty, bloody chick holding a kitten next to a tall man-boy who's dressed for class with his book bag, blue jeans, and a well-worn MSU T-shirt. I mean, it was an odd scene, but it was memorable.

For me, at least.

We talked about our families, our majors, and my obsessive love for cats. He laughed at me numerous times but in a sweet way that I was not used to. Marco made fun of me, but this guy seems to be intrigued with my humor and way of thinking. I tripped on the uneven pavement and almost ate it again. He stopped my fall. I liked his long arms. When I asked him his name, he replied, "Weston Drewbie, and you?" I laughed so hard that it scared the poor kitten, and I had to stop and adjust my hold on his tiny belly. "I know it's a funny last name, but damn, that laugh was savage!"

I stop in my tracks and turn to face him. I shrugged and gave him a half smile with eyebrows raised. "Well, you officially can't fall in love with me because we'll never get married." I state matter-of-factly, and I turn and begin walking once more.

"Whoa, whoa, whoa, not so fast. How you know that after a ten-minute walk? We haven't even traded our political and religious stances yet!" He catches up to me and stops me with a gentle hand.

I turned toward him and sighed, "My name is *Ruby*." I wait for him to get it.

He throws his face to the clouds and lets out a laugh that broke the silence but again scared the shit out of the kitten. He noticed my struggle and gently cradled the scared little guy and shook his head. "Ruby Drewbie." He laughed again. "And your middle name?"

"Leigh. After my Boom-ma. Ruby Leigh Brooks." I make sure to give him a second to linger in my eyes. "So as you can see, Ruby Drewbie is not a respectful name for anyone to have, so be careful with how hard you fall for me, sir," and I break his stare before he can break mine.

"Respectful name? Didn't you just say you were named after, was it, Boom-ma?"

"You better not talk about my Boom-ma!"

"Okay, we can talk about who takes whose name later, but first, what are you gonna call this little guy? I'm assuming if you almost died for him, you'll be keeping him?"

"Um, one hundred percent." I scratch the kitten's head and think about the name for a minute. Cats remind me of my dad. We always grew up with cats, and my mom never really liked them. When my parents divorced, Bitty Kitty went with my dad until he passed. He was gray like this little guy. After Bitty Kitty died, Dad let me get a kitten from the shelter, and I picked another gray male. I named him Pepper because I was ten, and every ten-year-old names their animal after an object it's closest in color to.

Tell me I'm wrong.

And now, this little guy has landed in my lap, a gray male kitten that came with a side of man-boy right when I needed love most.

As for the name, I think for a moment, and I remember one of my dad's favorite baseball players, and I say, "Mickey. His name's Mickey." I scratch his chin, and he leans into my love as if approving the name Mickey.

"Like the mouse?" he asked, and I scoffed.

"Heck no! Disney World is the ninth layer of hell to me. It's after Mickey Mantle. He's my dad's favorite baseball player of all time." I give Mickey a chin scratch.

"Well, Mickey, looks like this young lady right here just saved your life. Lucky boy." Weston took over the scratching for me, and Mickey did not mind at all. "Well, you and the little guy have a lot of connecting to do, so I'm going to leave you to it. I hope you have some Band-Aids in that house of yours. It was nice not seeing your brains splattered today." He smiled coyly and turned to go. "Maybe we'll run into one another again? I can't promise a kitten every time, though."

"No kittens, no promises," I say. "And thank you so much for your help."

"Anytime, Ruby Leigh. Anytime." He turned and walked down the driveway.

"Do you want a ride home?" The question sounded more desperate than helpful.

"No, ma'am, I prefer to walk. Plus, I've seen how you run, so I'm a bit concerned about your driving."

"Rude."

"I call 'em how I see 'em, Ruby."

"Don't you want my number?"

"Do you want to give it to me?"

"Maybe."

"When you're sure, come find me. I work on your running route."

"Where?"

"Maybe see you soon?"

"Wait, what? You're not going to tell me?"

"You're smart. I bet you'll figure it out." He turns and walks at a pace I know not to keep pushing.

We're having a moment, aren't we? Like, my own how-I-met-your-mother story! I know my self-sabotaging skills will ruin it somehow, but I'm grateful for the depression distraction in the meantime. I look at Mickey, and he looks back at me, and a purr begins to rumble in his tiny chest. "Well, Mickey, let's go introduce you to Joanna! Don't worry. We'll go find your new friend tomorrow." I kissed his nose, and he squinted his eyes in approval. I walked in the house and closed the door behind me.

Kittens make everything better.
And cute man-boys too, I guess.

CHAPTER 8

Wednesday, October 20, 2021

This morning, fall is in full swing, and it seemed to happen overnight like it always does. The leaves are a deeper shade of red and orange, and the air has an edge of coolness to it like when you feel the wave of colder air hit your face when you stand in front of an open freezer on a warm day. It's amazing to me how quickly things can shift. One day it's summer, and then *bam*, soup season's upon us.

Like in so many instances, life models nature, and I'm still adjusting to the sudden eviction of my eating disorder five years ago. The behaviors that once helped me survive my anxiety were taken from me before my brain was ready to be on its own, and it makes it difficult to stay on track in uncertain times. My bagel's been staring at me since the start of my planning, and the weight of its purpose is difficult to swallow today. Time to fact check: I have to eat. I need food. I can't let the days turn into months and then into years. Like the leaves that change without warning, I can be back in deep with my ED in 2.5 seconds with zero recollection on how I got there.

I love bagels. That's not the issue.

Although I know in my heart that Michael's proposition to Cam was merely a desperate cry for help, it's still hard not to take it personally. Again, I get it. He loves me and wants only me, but then, why did he hit on *her*. How can I convince my core that I'm enough? Marco made me feel this way for so long, and I stayed and took the blows one by one until the final knockout, and I'm still affected by it to this day. Is this the beginning of the end? Will Michael end up like Marco? Am I cosmically bonded to men who make me feel secure and loved and then screw me over?

"Shut up. Shut the hell up," I whisper to my ED. Acknowledging my disorder's presence helps me take control of my thoughts, and I take a bite of the bagel. I stand up, toss the rest of the pastry into the woods, and walk toward the building.

At least I took a bite. Small victories count in life, especially in mental illness.

*****

The air's cool and damp, and I can see the moon now as it replaces the sun in the gray sky. I made it through needy ninth graders' attention-seeking behaviors only to come home to the never-ending parenting duties I signed up for willingly. The good news? Michael came home at dinner, and I've been walking for the last two hours just trying to clear my head. I'm not surprised that I ended up in front of Cam's house for the third time. I'm drawn to her, and knowing now that Michael senses it too doesn't excuse his actions, but it helps explain them.

I remember a conversation I had with one of my marriage mentors a while back. I asked her what makes her marriage so strong, and she stated without hesitation, "My husband's my best friend. It's me and him against the world, and that's how it's gotta be to make it work." At the time, I didn't have a girlfriend to fall back on, so her request was easy enough. All I had was Michael, so there was no contest. Actually, that's a lie. I had my eating disorder too. My ED was my best friend for so long, there was no room for anyone else. Even Michael took a back seat to it if I'm honest.

It makes me wonder, did I keep my eating disorder so long because it was my only friend? That realization feels sad but accurate. I remember asking a counselor one time, "How am I supposed to just give it up?" It felt wrong, like I was abandoning a senior cat at the shelter because it lost its newness.

I'm sorry, ED.

Sometimes it's hard to think of my disorder as a parasite, not a companion. It was the only constant in my roller coaster of a childhood. I shake my head with a tension that comes from deep within. The rattle of my sinus cavity tickles my nose, and I wipe it with the back of my hand. I have to keep my wise mind thinking about it on those terms so I don't slip up and give it a room to rent in my head again.

I run my thumb across my left wrist over my Exodus 3:14 recovery reminder and the moon phases that Camryn and I got to match. They've faded a bit over time, but there's no removing the branding *or* their meaning. I've fought for my recovery daily since 2016, and for an eating disorder, that's exactly what it takes. It's the only addiction that you can't just give up completely. Think about it. When I had to give up running, I stopped it cold turkey. It was hard, but I made a conscious choice to stay out of trainers and off the roads. When food is a part of the addiction, it's unavoidable. Living things have to eat to survive, so instead of just giving up the disordered behavior, a person's expected to forget everything their body and brain's been doing for who the hell knows how long and *just eat normally*. Sounds easy to those who've never suffered, but it's torture to do opposite action when your whole body is telling you it's in danger.

The wind shifts, and I feel my heart actually ache in response. I've only felt this twice before, and I can picture the Marco- and Weston-shaped shadows left in my soul. Their silhouettes no longer have a frame, but their void feels like an old injury that flares up to remind me of my reckless days when I leapt without looking. Yes, they were boys that had my heart years ago, but once the heart is given away, it never comes back the same. That's the risk you take with loving someone.

I wonder if my shadow ever darkens their hearts?

Yesterday, Camryn texted me that she needed time to process how she wanted to move forward, and I'm trying to respect her wishes and give her the space and time she needs to figure it all out, but if I'm honest, the thought of losing her is terrifying. I can see her through the bay window reading Atticus's book of poetry that she loves so much.

"Love her, but leave her wild."

I get chills, and I move quietly to the wooden swing in the corner of the yard. It overlooks a serene little goldfish pond that the owner of the house built, and I always sit here when I need to get some space to think. Unfortunately, right now it's my best option of moving water, and I realize the pang in my heart to be on Sweetleaf grows daily.

I can feel the mist of the falls even now.

She must've felt my presence because I hear the screen door creak open and slam shut, and she's tiptoeing through the moon-lit grass leaving a footprint each time her foot softly leaves the earth. I can feel the tears stinging my eyes already just with the sight of her. She is barefaced and has her favorite tie-dye T-shirt on. She gently eases herself onto the swing next to me but doesn't say a word, and we sit there in silence. The tears that are stinging my eyes overflow onto my cheeks and then fall to my lap. I wipe them with my sleeve, not caring one bit about the mess or how it made my face even more raw, and I turn and look into her turquoise eyes. I can see they're brimming with tears too.

God, please give me the words.

I take a deep breath and let it out. She curls her lips into a slight forced smile saturated with concern, and she asks, "How're you doing?"

My lip quivers, and I part my lips to speak, but nothing comes out. I know what I want to say. I just have to find my voice. "There's just so much. I don't know where to start." My chin bounces up and down, and my teeth clink together so loud that I physically grab my jaw to help stop the quaking.

"Yeah, I know what you mean." We both know that we may never fully regain what we had, and that's why the tears come. Right or wrong, she became my person, and she's now slipping away.

I'm not ready to lose her, but I know what I have to do moving forward.

"How're *you* feeling?" I ask, afraid of the answer.

"Pissed off, actually. I'm just *so mad* at Michael. He's screwed everything up." The tears are flowing down her cheeks now too, and we are both staring straight ahead into the night. The moon phase is between waxing gibbous and full, so the yard is lit up, which makes the sadness seem more exposed.

"I'm sad, like big sad. I just don't know what to do next." I let the confession slip, and it seems juvenile, but it's the truth. "I'm so sorry this happened. I've figured out that

Michael's not in a good place, but that does not excuse his behavior toward you at all. I just wish I could have done something—*anything*—to avoid this."

"This is not on you, Ruby. This is on Michael. I've gone over the scenario *over and over* in my brain. I thought maybe I did something to give him the idea that *that* was what I wanted, or that I gave off the vibe that all three of us together was an actual option. And as hard as I try, I can't even think of *one* incident that would give him the idea that'd be appropriate to ask that of me. I just can't. I've been your best friend, your shoulder to cry on, your support, and you've done the same for me. So how'd he get it so *twisted?*" She shakes her head.

"And that's just it! I think he's intimidated by the fact that we *are* so close. Our whole marriage it's just been me and him, and he constantly threw himself into his work to avoid my chaos, but I was too consumed by my disorder to notice. Now that I'm more present and out of my head, he's been forced to check in, and I'm realizing how hard it's been for him. Regardless of all that, it didn't give him the right to offend you, betray me, *all* while messing up what we've built. It's just selfish and wrong." I look at her, and her face turns cold. She bites the inside of her lip as she always does when she's angry.

"I'm not sure I can forgive him, Ruby." She speaks what we both feel into existence.

"I know," I say, "but I have to find a way to."

She moves her hand over mine and whispers, "I know."

Camryn's my hero. She's faced abandonment, shame, and loneliness head on, yet she continues to grow more confident in her decisions and actions daily. When she told me that she was leaving her husband, I thought she'd lost her mind. I knew she was miserable, but I always thought they could work it out. I feared that she was choosing the harder road that had no guarantees of leading to the happiness she was seeking. Despite it all, she faced all her demons and pushed forward. I know she's glad she did.

I held Cam's hand throughout the whole divorce process, standing by her even when I didn't fully agree with all her choices because that's what best friends do. It was hard for me to accept that she was taking on my actual nightmare willingly, and it baffles me how she wasn't terrified to be on her own with Roe after being with her ex for so long. Well, here she sits, two years postdivorce, and she's doing it. It wasn't always easy, but she fought tooth and nail to get what she wanted and deserved in life. Camryn always told me that she's not afraid to take a risk if it means gaining happiness.

Divorce freed her.

It terrifies me.

Silence takes over as I let go of her hand in the moonlight. Camryn and I were star-crossed lovers from the start. We were never meant to be this intertwined, but our need for acceptance and love was so strong when we met. I was searching for security and strength after I gave up my ED, and she was learning to love and value herself outside of the views and values of the church. We were able to provide that for one another when we couldn't get it from within. I don't regret anything about our connection because even though the downfall of our friendship was inevitable, we helped each other survive a time that we may not have if we'd gone at it alone. Whether the struggle is disorder or divorce, it seems easier with someone who loves you in your corner. When the universe sends you a lifeline, you take it. Then when you're able, you let go of the rope.

Letting go of her hand feels scary, and I reach for it again, but she's pulled it out of reach. I look up to stop the

116

tears, and I see the shining moon. I know regardless of where life takes us, the moon will always remind me of Camryn.

She breaks the silence. "I know you are going to work things out with Michael, and I get it."

"Cam, I love you...so much, but he's my husband." A vision of sandy-blonde hair and scared blue eyes take over, and I suddenly long for my green blankie and Bitty Kitty. I have to work through this with him. He made a mistake, but I have to give him a chance to make it right. "He fought for me when I was killing myself, and he never gave up on me. Now I have to do the same for him." The words hurt as they came out, and I know they hurt Camryn too.

I saw the pain go straight to her heart, and with a nod, she said, "I know."

I hesitate. "I love you." My chest heaves and stops.

Her face breaks, and I see her pain, "I love you too."

It's funny when something comes to an end that you weren't expecting. There's a hole that is left in your soul with no transition time to prepare anything to fill it, so there is this gaping open wound susceptible to all the elements. My heart is *wounded*. There is a hole in it that will never be filled. It's *Cam's* hole. But I've survived with two holes in my heart so far.

Sometimes, I see them both in my dreams. Cam joined the cast of ghosts of Ruby's past last night. Her eyes are even more brilliant in my subconscious. I wonder if that's how it goes with true love. One just never quite heals from loss of it. I truly love Camryn, and saying this now feels like swallowing an entire wave.

"Cam, I gotta go."

"I know."

"I'm sorry."

"I know." She stands up, and she forces a smile.

"You'll always be my person." I stand to face her.

"Don't climb any trees," she teases.

"Don't stop sending me TikToks of cats."

"Deal."

"I love you, Cam."

"I love you too." She sways as she walks back through the dewy grass and disappears through the creaking screen door without looking back. The porch light goes off, and I hear the dead bolt click. Its latch symbolizes a finality that will haunt me in quiet moments when I least expect it. I take one last look at the moon tonight as if not to forget what it looks like from this space and time.

Goodbye, Cam.

I begin the short journey across the street that I've done so many times before, but this time, each step crumbles the vision I had of my future. It is maddening to be here again, losing someone I thought would be a part of my life forever.

I remember when Marco gave up on me. He was not willing to do what it took to heal our dysfunction, and he walked away without looking back. Weston had a choice too: Mississippi or us, and he chose the comfort of home over the risk of adventure. I honestly don't blame him. I was sick, and I couldn't see it. He did. Marco did too.

Maybe they're the smart ones.

I'm not angry at either of them for *not* choosing me. Marco had my teenage years and Weston my college years, but I was meant to be with Michael for a *lifetime*. From day one, I knew I had to make the choice to love him and only him. That's what true love is to me, a daily choice to see someone for who they *truly* are and do your best to help them feel safe and loved. It sounds cliché, but there's something about a choice that puts the ball in my court, and I can either choose to swing or drop the racket and quit.

I'm not a quitter.

I look up and see the shadows that hide the imperfections of the moon's surface. When it's full, the dips and the valleys that make it unique are displayed, while also highlighting its amazing size and stature. It seems to be a reminder to the world that even if you can't shine your full potential at all times, you're a masterpiece of the universe's design to shine when all the cosmos align, and even when the world can't see us, we still exist. I've always felt safer in the shadows, but now, I want to learn to live in the light.

The sun will always expose the moon's true form, and the universe will always divulge the depths of our souls. I don't want to be afraid of soul exposure anymore. There's such beauty in the breakdown, and I don't want to fear it. It's such a waste of energy to run from the truth because it's ultimately the one thing that sets us free from the demons we spend so much time trying to keep hidden in the shadows.

I want to bask in the light of the moon and dance in the warmth of the sun. My parents' divorce broke me as a child, but I pulled myself together. My eating disorder tried to take my life, but I fought the monster and came out victorious. I think about Ruiz's second agreement: "*don't take things personally.*" It's one of the hardest things to do when feelings and emotions are deeply connected to trauma and pain that still feel so raw no matter how much time has passed. It is the human condition to rise again and again out of the ashes, and I have made it this far, so there's no point in giving up *now*. I have to press on. I have to fully heal. The only other choice is suffering, and I'm done with suffering. It's time to make a shift. It's time to make a change. I know God has a plan. I just have to trust it.

I have to trust myself.

I make it back to our front yard, and I see sweet Murphie through the glowing window meowing like crazy. Her toe beans make a *squeak, squeak, squeak* on the glass as she slowly paws it in a desperate attempt to look cute and get me to come inside. I'm not ready to be in four walls, so I linger on the front step.

I know I have to continue to face my wolves. This situation has proven to me that I still have fears that can cause me to derail at any moment, and I have to continue to keep my high beams on and my hands on the wheel.

The risk of losing my family is now greater than my disordered thoughts, and I close my eyes and address the black beasts, *You have no power here anymore, wolves. I have nothing else to lose.* And for once, that's a freeing statement instead of a death sentence. My best friend is gone. There's no way to go back. My husband is broken. He needs my support. My kids need a mom. I refuse to let them down. Murphie wants snuggles. *I have to go inside.*

I take a step toward the threshold, and I'm surprised by Michael's shadow silhouette standing in the newly opened doorway. He doesn't say anything. He closes the door behind him, walks to the first step, and sits down in the moonlight. He leaves a space for me, and I take the invitation. There's a long silence, and I'm thankful for it. There are no words right now to describe how broken my heart is, and Michael knows it. The wind blows my long brown hair onto his shoulder, and he carefully brushes it behind my ear, lingering his finger on my neck. The electricity buzzes down my spine, and I shudder. I gently lay my head on his familiar chest, and he engulfs me with his strong hold as he squeezes me into his body with a thankfulness I can feel to my core. I know this gratitude. I had the same desperate relief when Michael held me the night before he took me to the Manna House. It's a mix between disbelief and honor that someone could see the ugliest side of your humanness and still actually want to hold you.

That's true love.

True love is terrifying. It's terrifying because it's so beautiful that the thought of losing it can lead one to not even attempt to attain it in the first place. I saw true love that stormy night on Watson's Place as my parents embraced, and the next day, I saw it shatter like a wine glass that slipped silently through an unassuming grasp and crash to the ground with no way to piece it back together again. All you can do is call it a loss and get a new glass with new wine. The problem is that like wine, love leaves stains that can never be removed. The more glasses you let fall, the more stains you have to live with, and I'm not willing to live with the stain of a failed marriage to a man whom I still love more than life itself. He's messed up, but so have I, *many times*, and he didn't throw me out and start over with a shiny new glass of wine. He got on his hands and knees and didn't hesitate to help me pick up my broken pieces.

Now it's my turn to hold the broom.

His grip tightens around my shoulder, and I'm thankful for his strong hold. It's a physical reminder that this will not be easy, but nothing in life worth having is, and Michael's worth fighting for.

"Mama? Daddy?" I was so invested in my thoughts that I didn't even hear the door open behind us. Suddenly, we are drenched in the light of the living room, exposed like the full moon, and I turn to see Hudson's face questioning the scene he's stumbled upon. "Are you guys okay? Why are you sitting outside?" His face is full of concern, and I know that he is going to need reassurance.

"Yeah, bud, we're fine. Daddy and I are just admiring the beautiful moon. It's almost full! You know what that means? Completion and transformation!" Michael sucks in a sob, and I pat the empty space next to me, and Hud takes the invitation gladly. Instead of sitting on my right, he barrels straight forward and wedges his way right smack-dab in the middle of Michael and me, and we both grin as his head replaces mine on his chest. My mind floats back to the lightning-filled night I watched my parents embrace. Their ugly was being exposed right before my eyes, but all I saw was love. Kids are often asked to endure adult scenarios with no explanation or understanding of how to navigate them. As I comb my fingers through Hudson's hair, I'm overcome with emotion. I silently wipe the tears from my eyes and catch Michael's gaze once more. Tears are flowing down his cheeks as well, and I know this is a full-circle moment in my life. I'm at peace with what I need to do next.

I'm not going to let you down, Hudson Blue.
I promised you that a while back.
And I intend on keeping it.

CHAPTER 9

Thursday, June 22, 2006

June

I see the steam pouring out of the small, closet-sized bathroom, and The Fray is blaring with Weston singing along with the lyrics as he scrubs his beautifully exposed body through the tempered glass.

He is so damn sexy.

Turns out, I did find the hot kitten hero—the very next day, actually! Mainly because I stalked Main Street for hours, pretending to do sprints, but I wasn't fooling anyone. The grouchy owner of Whisky Blues even put a bottle of water out on the front steps in both kindness and spite. I'm pretty sure he just didn't want me to die on his property. Weston showed up at his parent's shop to open it up fifteen minutes late. I was reluctantly consuming the water on the bar's steps.

I jumped up, trotted down the stairs, and jogged right past the storefront and acted as if I didn't even notice him.

"Ruby Brooks?"

His chocolate curls were still damp, I assume from a morning shower. His polo was tight in all the right places, and I suddenly realized I must look like crap compared to his attire.

"Weston? Hey! Sorry, I didn't see you."

"You found me," he teased.

"You wish! I was just on my normal run this morning. You just happen to be on my route."

"Lucky me. Want to come in and have a cup of coffee? I see you peddled some water from Bill."

"Yeah, I'm not so sure it's safe to drink. That man despises me."

"He hates life in general. Don't take it personally."

"Well, I guess I can spare a minute before I have to get back for class."

"You go to class?"

"Of course. Don't you?"

"When necessary."

"Well, I love learning. It makes life interesting."

"You're interesting."

"You have no idea. You remember our agreement, though, right? You're not allowed to fall in love with me."

"I said unless I can't help it." He held the store door open for me as I walked in under his outstretched arm.

I didn't make it to class that morning.

Now, here we are, almost three years later, playing our roles as college singles with little responsibility before life gets really complicated. And I know it will get complicated, but my newfound happiness has served me well. My anxiety is masked by adventures, music, starvation, serotonin created by long runs, wild sex, and the love of a cat. And my body image is reflected from my ED's satisfaction and Weston's adoring perception, and as if on cue, he turns from the flowing water toward me with hungry eyes. I feel my pulse between my legs, and the jolt of adrenaline makes my heart beat faster and faster. There's a high I get from sex that comes even when I don't. Its more about pleasing him that gets me off than anything else. He pulls his chin over the shower door and smiles his charming toothy grin, and I'm done.

God, I want him.

He turns his head to receive the water, and he allows the stream to fill his mouth as he runs his hands through his wet chocolate curls. I imagine his hands on my waist lifting me easily into his possession with ease. Although I have many meaningless hookups to compare Weston to, it's really Marco's standard that's being shattered with every encounter we share. Marco's touch was selfish and exploratory. Weston's touch is intentional and experienced. The two can't be compared.

I went through a wild phase in the summer after high school. I was a mastermind of flirtation, and my childlike frame gives guys some kind of sick I-could-throw-you-across-the-room fantasy that's hard to shake, so I used my sex appeal to my advantage in getting over the devastation of the loss of my first love. If my time as a woman has taught me anything, it's that my body is a concert that men will pay *any* amount to have all access. If there's a glimmer of hope that the VIP pass to *my* show was on the table, they would come to will call with all the resources in their disposal to get that ticket.

I'd been held down in a toxic relationship since I was twelve, so looking back, especially with my history of only feeling useful when I was pleasing someone else, my summer-before-Freshman-year hoedown was inevitable. The irony here? I still hated my body, yet I exposed it to any guy who was willing to praise it as is. I was like a dog that would sit, shake, and roll over for the least amount of attention, and I felt sick over my actions. For years, I had tried and tried to be exactly what Marco wanted, and no matter what I did, it was never good enough.

Trading morality for attention is not something I recommend, but I don't regret being with the guys I was with at the time. However, I do regret leading them to believe that they had a chance beyond the one-night stand. But no matter how right or wrong, my God, I lived for their wanting me. I began to get a reputation around my high school friends, but I didn't care. It didn't bother me what people I'd be leaving thought about me and my promiscuity. I was escaping to Mississippi, and it was going to be with a middle finger up to the in the rearview mirror for sure.

I promised myself that I would be single once I got to MSU, and I did pretty well at first. Joanna's introverted ways helped that for sure, but then I almost got hit by a car, found a cat, and a guy all in one swoop.

Before we head out, I'm gonna need an anxiety release.

Perks of dating an addict, I guess you could say!

I slip off the bed and ease my thong down to my ankles. Weston's full attention has shifted from the shower to me as he continues to let the water from the head rush his throat, and it makes me ache for his tongue. His lips are full and soft, and I want to feel them on my skin. I pull his Rolling Stones T-shirt off, and as the cotton slowly brushes my nipples, they become the directorial beacons that pull me with gravity-like force to the shower and the man inside it.

As I approach, he turns and presses his body against the glass. I look at him long and hard before I move any closer. I never knew that the human body could be both imperfect and still sexy all at the same time. Marco was chiseled, hard, and almost too beautiful to touch. He was either sore from training or needing to train, so sex was fast and furious with a lot of grunts, grabs, and sweat. It was basically a workout with a happy ending.

It's not like that with West. He's different. Having sex with him is playful, sweet, and fulfilling. And I was more than happy to offer him a VIP pass anytime he wanted it.

He backed off the glass and let it fog up once again. I waited, and he pressed his finger on the glass and slowly, methodically, wrote, "*Join me?*" It made my heart jump, and I stepped back to the sink.

Two can play at this game.

I took the shaving cream next to the faucet, and I wrote, "*Come and get me.*" Before I could finish the last E, Weston flung open the glass and snatched me up with ease. He firmly gripped my hips and pressed me up against the cold tile with the perfect amount of pressure to make my body ache for more.

"Got ya."

"Not fair. You have like a six-foot-five wingspan."

"Quit talking basketball. You're turning me on."

"I hate basketball!"

"I love you."

"Not allowed."

"I don't know how not to."

He slipped his tongue between my lips, forcing me to let him in. I allowed the tip of my tongue to tease him, and it felt weird to trust someone again. I allowed him to fill my mouth with warmth in a shower that had turned freezing with the overuse. As the icy water pounded my hands on his exposed back, the tiles felt rough and smooth on mine. He only released his grip for a split second to place his dick between my thighs that were a whole other kind of wet with anticipation. He slips into me with ease and gives me three big thrusts before he steps back and slams his back on the glass, forcing it to fling open so hard that I was sure it would bust. He made a few long strides toward the bed, and with the perfect amount of force, he landed on top of me as he dug me deeper into the comforter. He held my face in his palms and looked into my soul as he continued to show me what selfless sex feels like as he made me feel valued, worshiped, and wanted all at once. Lovemaking like this makes me want to apologize to anyone I'd fucked before because what I am experiencing with Weston is nothing like the desperate attempts to fake connection for a shameful self-esteem boost.

Once I'm about to climax, I grab his firm ass and pull him into me as deep as he can go. Orgasms are second best part of sex for me, and that's if I actually achieve the difficult task of actually getting there. The highlight for me is satisfying the guy so he doesn't need to go elsewhere for pleasure. When they grunt, thrust, and shake, I feel powerful and in control.

I need to be in control.

After Weston reaches his peak, he puts his lips close, and they brush my ear as he whispers, "Ruby Brooks, I want to hold you forever."

"Don't say that, West."

"It's how I feel."

"Feelings change."

"Not feelings like these." He was stroking my arm that I had laid across his broad chest. His eyes were pleading, begging for me to reciprocate the sentiment, but I can't.

"We'll see."

"You've got to let me in, though, Rube."

"Let you in? You were just in my vagina. How much more *in* can you be?"

"Relationships are about more than sex. You're my best friend. I've never felt this way before. You're special, Ruby. I wish you could see that."

I didn't reply. I leapt out of bed to take over the shower and wash the domestic off of me. There is an elephant in the room that we don't like to discuss: graduation is coming, and I'm mountain bound as soon as I get my diploma. As for Weston, the family store is his future. His mom says so.

I'm afraid to admit it, but I love Weston. It's a balanced, healthy love that I feel equally valuable in, yet I can't bring myself to accept it. I tried to change my wants and needs when I was with Marco to make him happy and fulfilled. I'm not ready to do that with Weston—or anyone, for that matter. People disappoint you and leave. That's how it goes. If I'm going to hate myself, I want to do it in a climate I love. I can't stand the flat farmland for much longer.

I hear a familiar faint scratching at the shower door. This time, it's not Weston. I hate that after all this time they can still find me.

*****

December

I look out the window of my bedroom into the gray sky mirroring the gray cotton plant skeletons in the distance that were recently tilled into the gray dirt in anticipation for the planting season. Weston ran to pick up food while I stayed back to get my final run in for the day. I hear the familiar trill of a text message notification, and I turn in the direction of the noise. It's his phone, and I realize he's left it on my desk.

I look at Mickey, and I ask, "Should we see who it is?" He just glares at me with apathy stronger than the seniors I'm currently student teaching, and I ignore his grouchiness and head to the phone. They say curiosity killed the cat, but they never said it kills relationships. I think that saying is old as dirt. Its creator clearly never had text messaging.

It was a message from Mama Drewbie: "*Weston, Dad and I are so proud of you for taking over the store. We know you won't regret it. Cheers to new beginnings.*"

I slammed the phone down on the wood so hard that it cracked.

He's taken over the store?

Without telling me?

I sink on my bed as Mickey nudges my elbow with his wet nose. He forces his way into my lap and stares at me with his green eyes. I'm too numb to move, and I'm too sad to cry. I feel the anxiety creeping up my chest and manifesting itself in the corners of my heart that only know this type of deep pain. Weston was never going to come to North Carolina with me. He told me he wasn't. His plan from the beginning was to take over the store for his parents, and no one will change that.

Not even me.

The text washes over my brain like a wave licking the sand after a storm, slowly, methodically just begging to be forgiven for the destruction it's caused. "*Cheers to new beginnings.*" I've been kidding myself these past few years. It's like trying to will the last Starburst in the pack to be pink even though it's clearly orange. No matter how much you wish it was pink, orange is what you're left with. Take it or leave it.

Sucks to be the orange Starburst in this metaphor.

Crazy to think that Weston did exactly what he said that he was going to do, and yet I'm *still surprised* as if this is new information when I've known it was a part of the script all along. Our ending was stated in the prologue. I just chose not to read it. I've learned that avoidance doesn't change the plot. It merely exposes hidden pain that's picked over like the rotten fruit that's been left to decay on the vine. At some point, you have to prune the plants so that new growth has room to flourish, but it's hard to pick through the fruit that could have been if only it were discovered sooner.

Just then, Weston bursts through the door, and I jolt as the slam of the door brings me to the present. His hands are full of to-go bags from the restaurant up the street, and his toothy grin fades when he sees the demeanor of mine.

"Woah, Rube, who licked the red off your candy cane?"

"Your mom texted you."

"Oh, really?" He shifts his weight onto the other food and puts the plastic bag on the counter in preparation. "Did you read it?"

"Yes, I read it."

"What did she have to say?"

"That we should raise a toast for you."

"Oh, Rube. I was gonna tell you tonight."

"It's fine. We knew this day was coming."

"You can stay here with me, Rube. We can make this work."

I see the desperation in his eyes, but my heart is already beginning to harden as if I'd looked into Medusa's unforgiving eyes. "Let's not talk about it, okay?"

"We have to at some point."

"Well that some point doesn't have to be tonight."

"But if not now, then when? We're running out of runway, Rube."

Run.

"Speaking of run." I push Mick off my lap and jump into my Nikes next to the bed.

"I said runway, not *run*. Come on, Rube, not now."

"I totally forgot while you were gone. I won't be long."

"The food'll be cold."

"Go ahead and eat and put mine in the fridge. I'll heat it up when I get back."

When I got back, Weston was gone, and the food was in the fridge. I slipped off my sweaty clothes, scooched in bed next to Mickey, and fell asleep to Fleetwood Mac in my head singing, "Would you stay if she promised you heaven? Would you ever win?" If I actually ask myself the question, would Weston ever win with me?

The answer is a clear, resounding no. How could he? I don't know how to win with myself.

My mom once said, "You're not a band of gypsies, so quit acting like it." At the time, I think she was referring to a water balloon fight that broke out between siblings, but the phrase stings more now more than it did in the original scolding. I'm not as loveable as I claim to be, and I need to quit pretending like I am. Why would Weston leave his mapped-out, silver-platter life to take the road less traveled with me?

I can almost see Frost's yellow wood.

My fantasy: life in the mountains. My reality: the flat farms of Mississippi. The sweat on my back is drying, and the sheets are grossly peeling off of my skin as I roll on my stomach. A howl outside my window makes goose bumps pop up on my thighs, and a tingling erupts in my lower back as the adrenalin hits my heart. I place a pillow over my head and let the emotional tsunami come as I stand on the shore waiting for impact. I don't duck. I don't try to escape. I just dig my toes deeper and deeper into the sand so I can get my footing.

CHAPTER 10

Friday, March 4, 2007

January

My feet pound to a stop at the normal driveway that signals the finish line, and the tingles begin in my toes and travel to my heels. I rest my hands on my head and let the vapor escape my mouth without reservation. My hips are sore from the workout, but I'm thankful it's done. I yank at my leggings because they're falling down, and I notice Weston holding two mugs, sitting at the edge of the grass near the garage. He's in his sweats and hoodie, and I can see his toothy grin from three houses down. Dawn's glow is illuminating the bare fields in the distance, and I take a big breath in to regain my normal breathing rhythm. I let it out slowly, and the tingles in my feet dissipate.

It's depressing how quickly the runner's high passes.

"Hey, Ruby Brooks, how's the streets of Starkville this mornin'?"

"Empty, as always." I sit down next to him and cross my legs.

As the top of the sun peaks the horizon, he whispers in the space between us, "I could watch the sunrise with you forever."

"Gonna be beautiful up in NC. I'll send you pictures." I give him a wink, and his smile fades, and he turns away. I look at the steadily brimming ball of orange growing brighter and brighter, changing the black of the sky to dark blue, to deep red, and then to blood orange. It's surprising to me how quickly the sun seems to move when it rises versus its slow travel the rest of the day. I know the orbital speed doesn't change, but *still*. The most beautiful scene of the sun's performance happens so fast. Blink your eyes twice and it's too late. I'm always left wishing it would linger just a bit longer.

All good things have to come to an end.

Weston stands up, and his dark silhouette against the rising sun has a haunting feel to it. I turn and look at the broken cotton stalks stripped bare and begging to be tilled. I can sense his stare, but I'm afraid to face what I feel coming.

"Rubes, you know I can't leave Mississippi. My whole family's here. I'm officially taking over one hundred percent of the store in May. If I left, my mom would..." The last part hits him deep, and I know he truly can't imagine leaving the life plan his parents have wanted so desperately for him since he was young. Weston loves to travel and go on adventures, and what his parents are asking him to commit to goes against his true self, but he's too afraid to tell them what *he* wants. He's destined to run the store, and that is it. No other options were ever on the table. I have questioned that since day one, and his mother hates me for it.

The feeling's mutual.

"It's just so infuriating, Weston. You know that store is going to kill every dream you have of seeing the world and living the life we dream about. You're not *stuck* in Starkville. I just wish you'd talk to them." I suggest for the hundredth time, and he turns to face the rising sun as his hands comb through his messy hair. "Don't blow this off, Drewbie. You know I'm right."

"Dammit, Ruby, don't you think I know that?" he scoffed. "Not everyone can just up and run off like you did, and look at you." He looked me up and down as I stood to defend myself because I know where the conversation is heading, "You're sick, Rube, like *really* sick. You literally eat *nothing* but *plain tuna* and then run yourself *to death* daily. Anytime I bring you food, into the fridge it goes until it starts to stink, and then you throw it in the garbage to stink until I come over and take it out. Don't think I don't see it, Rube. I'm so damn scared I'm going to find you on the side of the road again and not in the cute-rom-com way we met that first day. No, it will be with ambulances, sirens, and tears, Ruby—my tears because you'll be *dead!* Your heart is literally going to give out, and you just keep on *running*. You've *got* to start eating."

He's trying to shift the conversation onto me, and I'm sick of my eating disorder being the scapegoat for all the men in my life.

"My heart's *fine.*"

"Yeah, right, Ruby. I've seen you get up at night and do jumping jacks. It's stopping, isn't it? Your heart? Can you feel it?"

"The doctor said that forty beats per minute is normal for athletes that train as much as I do, and *you know* I can't eat before a run. I'll puke! Just forget it, Weston."

"I'm scared you won't stop until you kill yourself."

"Why do you care? I won't be here for you to see it."

"Ruby, I'm serious. I think you need help."

"You're just stuck on pleasing your mother."

"Quit changing the subject, Brooks. Did you hear me? You need help."

The corners of my mouth begin to curl down and quiver. "Leave."

"Ruby."

"Leave, Weston."

"Really?"

"Really."

"Damn, Ruby. So that's it? Just like that?"

"Goodbye, Weston."

He took the last sip of his coffee and placed the mug on the ground at my feet. He reached in his pocket for his keys and flipped them around three times and caught the whole lot in his grip. "You can't run from this forever, Ruby, whatever *this* is." He scans me up and down, and I want to hide.

"I said *leave!*" My voice cracks, and I turn for the door. I see Mickey in the window, and he's fuming that we're conversing without him present. His white belly is exposed as his paws stretch as high as they can reach with his meows silenced by the window between us. Tears are brimming my eyelids, and my chin begins to shake.

"Ruby, I'll always love you. I don't know how not to." He turns to get in his Cherokee. The door slams, and the engine rumbles to a start. Exhaust from the tailpipe creates a smoke that engulfs his vehicle as he backs out of the driveway, and then he leaves the cloud behind as he drives into the morning light. He's now an afterthought like the sunrise.

If people mean it when they say they love me, then how the hell is it so easy to leave me?

You know who doesn't leave me?

The wolves.

I can always count on them.

*****

March

The air is thin this chilly morning, and I'm lacing up my Nikes to hit the pavement. If I start my run now, I'll have two hours before I need to shower in time for class. The air is crisp, and my body's shivering as I stand up and look in both directions. I can see my breath, and it feels good to be cold. It makes me think of North Carolina. There's no cars in sight, so I start my stopwatch and press play on my iPod shuffle. It's tiny, and that's what I like about it. I can't stand anything weighing me down on my runs.

The less, the better.

I get an instant high as I feel the ache as the freezing air hits the back of my throat. The rhythm that I create with my consistent pace is addicting, and I know that this run will give me the mental strength I need to face the day. I can't concentrate when I skip my morning run. The sun won't make its appearance until about 6:27 a.m., so I have plenty of darkness. It's kind of odd, but I prefer to run in the dark. There's a danger factor that gets my adrenaline flowing, and I get a better workout when I'm a little afraid. Joanna says that it's the *dumbest shit she's ever heard*, but she just doesn't understand.

I have to run. The faster, the better.

I do my regular route down Maxwell to University Drive to Main. I see the bagel shop's open light buzzing, but other than that, I have the town to myself this early in the morning, and I prefer it that way. I shuffle my way through Dave's set list from the New Year's show, and the world and my problems disappear more and more as my feet take me for miles and miles. That's the beautiful thing about running. It's an escape like no other I've ever experienced. If I'm stressed, I run. If I'm anxious, I run. If I'm sad, I run. Once

I'm in the zone of my music and my memorized route, every-thing else in my brain just gets quiet, and I'm *free*. I can only feel peace when I'm pushing myself to my physical limits, and it has been even worse since I broke up with Weston for simply stating the truth.

I need help.

We faded as fast as we ignited. Like the sunrise, we were spectacular while we lasted, but some beauty can only last for *so* long. We both knew from the beginning that our dreams for a future together were never going to match up, so no matter how much love there was between us, the reality of our future together was always as clear as the French Broad that runs nightly through my dreams. We'd never be more than two ill-fated college lovers, and that was hard for me to swallow. Now, as I'm running alone, the sudden wave of emotion engulfs me all over again, like it's done every day since we called it quits. I run faster and harder to numb the pain.

*****

An hour into my run, as I'm making my way back down Main Street, I feel a sharp pain in my chest, and it stops me in my tracks. I double over at the waist, one hand on my breast in a desperate attempt to locate the problem as the other arm supports my upper half against my knee weakly. My breath quickens, and I begin to hyperventilate. I see stars dancing in the atmosphere in front of me, and I know I'm about to pass out. This happened the other night after my run, and I had to stumble into the closest bar for help. Thank goodness my buddy Warren was there. He insisted on taking me to hospital, but I refused, shook it off, and walked home in the dark.

This pain is intense. I sit down on the curb. I put my head between my knees and try to will it away, but I must've passed out. When I came to, the sun was peeking out from the horizon, and there was a small crowd of sunrise walkers hovering over me. One older man helped me sit up, and I put my hands behind me for support.

"Youn' lady, you al'rite? Joe here saw ya laid out on the sidewalk as he roun'ed the corner, and he called 9-1-1. They're on their way. What's ya name, darlin'?" The kind man knelt down so that his face was on my level, and I suddenly felt a wave of embarrassment about the whole situation.

"It's Ruby. Please call off the ambulance. I'm fine! I had a pain in my side—a runner's stitch, that's all! I'm fine." I tried to stand to prove my stability, but my legs failed me, and I succumbed to gravity. As I sit once more on the curb, the stars begin dancing in the space between me and the man insisting that I get checked out, but the world went black again before I got a chance to make my shameful exit.

*****

I woke up in the Oktibbeha County Emergency Room with a foggy head, tubes hooked up to my arms, and a monitor on my chest. The sounds of beeping sent panic through my veins, and suddenly, I'm seven years old, watching the wolves pace my bedside with no way to escape. I try to sit up, but the pain in my head forces me to lie back down. I hear the squeak of rubber on the slick hospital floors, and I try to will them into my room with a subconscious prayer.

How did I even get here?

As if on cue, a nurse named Ellen came through the door with a smile as big as her teased hair, and she exclaimed, "Oh, hey, honey! Nice to fin'ally see those pretty blue eyes of yours! I've been waitin' for you to wake up! Don't worry, doll, We got your dad on the phone a while back, and he should be here any minute! He was *really* concerned, but I told him that I wouldn't leave ya!" She busied herself checking all my vitals without skipping a beat, but I was still in shock.

"Ma'am, I'm sorry, but I'm confused." I shift my weight in the uncomfortable bed, and I try to get my bearings, "My dad's coming? Who called him?" I close my eyes and wince in pain. It has become increasingly difficult to get comfortable when I sit or lie down because of the lack of meat protecting my bones, but that is the least of my concerns at the moment.

"Honey, you passed out on Main right smack-dab in the middle of the morning crowd! All the walkers were walkin', and the storekeepers were settin' up shop fer the day, but you, my dear, had other plans! Lucky for you, your friend Weston was opening the store for his folks across the street, and he followed the ambulance here to make sure you're okay. Great young man. Great family! Been buy'n my husband's suits at their store fer thirty years now! He called your dad, and now here we are! Would you like fer him to come back? I told him I would let him know when you woke up." Before I had a chance to protest, Ellen half sprinted out the door to the waiting room to get Weston, and my heart monitor began to beat faster. I looked at the machine. My pulse had jumped to fifty-four, which is racing for me. I closed my eyes tight and attempted to will myself to the woods, but it didn't work. The wolves had me surrounded.

I heard a familiar knock, and I looked up to see Weston's toothy grin. He leaned hesitantly into the doorframe, holding his weight with the palms of his hands, but I could tell that he was scared to enter. We hadn't ended on the best of terms, and we've successfully avoided one another until now.

Why'd he have to be right?

"Hey there, Rube."

The familiar greeting stings, and my chin begins to chatter, and I pull the covers up over my chest.

"Sorry, I just don't know what to say." He confesses as he scoots a chair next to the bed, and with one smooth swoop, he gently moves my gross hair out of my eyes.

"How about *I told you so*? That seems appropriate enough." I trace back over the strand of hair that he moved. I'm not ready to feel his touch and lose it all over again.

"I wish I wasn't right, Ruby. You scared the hell out of me and half of the elder population in Starkville. Even Bill came out to check on you." He shakes his head. "I hate seeing you like this, Ruby. I truly do." He sat back abruptly in the chair after seeing me balk at his touch, but he didn't leave. I wish he would. There is no honor in starving and running myself to the point of passing out.

"Why'd you call my dad?" I asked, but I really didn't care about the answer. Picking a fight was better than suffering in awkward silence.

"Because, Rube, you could've *died*. Your damn heartbeat was like thirty! They were about to start CPR! I sure as hell wasn't gonna wait and call him until you were actually *dead!*" He sniffed back a sob, and I suddenly wanted to hold him. "You could've died, Ruby, right in my arms. How could you be so *blind* to it? Do you even care that you're a fucking skeleton, like *literal skin and bones* and *still* running? I don't get it."

Tears sting my eyes, and I pull the sheet up to my face to stop them from flowing. I feel the wrinkles on my cheeks, which are a sign of significant malnutrition, and close my eyes to disappear, but the world goes on, and I'm still here unfortunately.

Is that what I'm doing, trying to disappear? The less of me there is, the less pain I'll feel. The less of me there is, the less my anxiety will dictate my days and haunt my nights. The less of me there is, the less it will matter when I'm gone.

Am I suicidal?

But like a deranged, prolonged suicidal?

Better not say that out loud.

"You don't have to be here right now. You made your choice clear months ago."

"So now you are blaming me? Is it my fault for having a plan for my life that doesn't match up with yours? So damn sorry. And what a low blow. You're gonna blame me for your lack of common sense with food and exercise? Is that my fault too?"

"No, I never said that." My voice trails, and I look up. "I'm in this bed due to my own choices. I just don't know how to choose differently."

"Ruby Leigh, my girl!" Suddenly, my dad burst through the doorway and dropped to his knees at my bedside, tears already streaming down his cheeks. He's probably been crying ever since he left Atlanta. His suffocating embrace was comforting after feeling like I might float right out of the hospital bed since I woke up. "Ruby, my God, I'm so glad you are okay. Are you okay?" His hug got even tighter.

"Yeah, Dad. I'm sorry you had to come all the way here. I'm fine. Just passed out, that's all." I squirm a little in his grasp. I hate lying, especially to him.

"This isn't fine, Ruby. This is not fine at all. Patricia and I are so worried. She's in the waiting room. And *you*. You look… Ruby, are you on drugs? Weston, is she on drugs?" He looks from me to Weston for answers, but I know he is not ready to hear the truth. Weston's eyes meet mine, and I know I have to confess.

Daddy, I need you.

"No, Dad, I'm not on drugs. *I wish* that was it!" I laugh a little, but his crystal-blue eyes continue to pierce my soul for answers. I have avoided this conversation for at least a year. I have made excuse after excuse on why I couldn't come home over the various breaks. Summer school was easy, for starters, because I *always* took classes to get ahead. Then I went to Thanksgiving with the Drewbies, and that kept me in Mississippi until Christmas. Over winter break, we traveled to Vail to ski with our buddy Austin. He got us free lift tickets since he works there every summer, and I already had the gear passed down from a friend. Then the breakup happened, and that took a toll, so Dad and my stepmom Patricia reluctantly gave me the space I asked for. If he'd known that I was struggling with eating, he would have never stayed away.

Anorexia sucks.

"I'm not laughing, Ruby. There's nothing funny about this." He wiped his tears from his cheeks without blinking. His classic Russell Brooks stare was in full effect, and I wanted to be anywhere but in a hospital room with these two men. One of them loves me more than himself, and the other chose himself over me. Either way, I'm letting them down.

"I know, Dad. I'm sorry. I didn't know how to tell you." I try to fix my ponytail to be more presentable, but it's a lost cause. I hate how people in the movies look so good in the hospital bed. It's so unrealistic. I look how I feel—like *shit*.

"You talk to the ones that can help you, Ruby. It's bad enough that you have been hours away from us for years, but to hide from your family when you need us most. Oh, Ruby, I'm sorry I didn't come sooner. I should've known." The last line is not even for my ears, but he spoke his disappointment in himself out loud, and it made it all hurt even more.

"How could you know, Dad? This has *nothing* to do with you *or* the family."

"My daughter killing herself is not my business? Ruby, you're coming home as soon as we can get you out of here. Home is where you need to be." He stood up and looked around as if he would find some kind of sign-out sheet and we could be on our way. "When was the last time the doctor saw you? And the nurse, where is she?" He was pacing, and it was only making me more anxious.

"Dad, sit down. The nurse was just in here, and she said the doctor will make her rounds soon. No need to disrupt them. I'm fine." I swallow hard. "And, Dad, I'm not going home. Graduation is in two months, and I can't miss a day of student teaching. They'll make me start all over again in the fall, and that's *not* happening." I mean what I say, and he knows he can't stop me. He has never been able to. I'm a force to be reckoned with when I have my mind set. Just two years ago, he stood in front of my car to stop me from driving back to Mississippi through Hurricane Ivan. I'd gone home for the weekend, but Weston's PIKE formal was that night, and I refused to wait out the storm and miss the fun. I savagely put it in reverse, drove through the yard, jumped the curb, and drove into the dark clouds that loomed in the west. I never admitted it to him, but I was terrified the whole way to State. I love storms, but this one made the hairs on the back of my neck stand up. The air was thick, and I could feel the electricity with every strike of lightning. I saw two cars get smashed by trees, but I made it safely. Somehow, I always do.

I've always been a storm.

"Weston, thank you again for calling me. I'm so glad you were there. I truly am." He sniffs loudly and turns to look out the window to avoid eye contact. His eyes are weary, and it breaks my heart to see him so relieved. The drive here must've been unbearable. "Well, I'm going to find Pat, and I will be back." Weston nodded with respect, and Dad took his exit.

"See, Ruby? They care. They love you. They need you. And you need them." He is right, but I don't want to hear it. I want help, but here I'm now hating them for offering it to me. I'm not stable, and I know it. The question is, what do I do next? Sometimes the vast options that lay ahead of me are so many that I can't imagine picking only one. It's easier to sabotage any chance I might have in the future so that I can't be hurt when it doesn't go my way. How messed up is that?

Fear of failure is real.

"You can leave now, Weston. My dad's here. Are you happy? He gets to see the dumpster fire his daughter is in, isn't that what you wanted? Did you invite your mom here too? I'm sure she would love to see me laid up in bed dying. Why'd you even bring me here? You should've just let me die. That way, you'll be the hero, and I'll be the villain." When it comes out of my mouth, I instantly regret it. My desperate statement sounds juvenile because deep down, I know he made his choice months ago.

"That's not fair, Rube, and you know it." He stands, and pauses on the way out the door. "I'll always love you. I don't know how not to. Take care of yourself, Ruby Leigh Brooks. You're getting exactly what you deep down wished for this whole time: for me to leave. You aren't the victim of lack of love. I hope you see that. You're a victim of your own mind, Rube, and I can't make you want to get better." And just like that, he was gone. I saw Dad and Pat coming down the hallway, and they casually waved at Weston as they crossed paths, clueless that it would be their last. He turned around one last time, and I wiped a tear away from my face.

I try to perk up as Pat comes to give me a hug. She's quietly sobbing, and her embrace is unexpected and warm. I love Patricia. She is the one good thing that came from my parents' divorce. She never had children of her own, but she's always loved Charleigh and me so well from day one. "We were so worried," she gasped. "Oh, Ruby." And she didn't have to say anymore. I knew what she was thinking. Her hands moved from around my protruding shoulders to covering her mouth.

"I've discovered the secret to weight loss," I try to joke, but again, it's a tough crowd.

"Ruby, that's enough." Her mascara was running down her face, and I felt the guilt creep up my throat like a pill that refuses to go down.

"I'm sorry. I just really don't know what to say." It's the truth, for once. I had been in a web of lies with my family for so long now that I didn't even know the truth from the lies.

"Hello. Mr. and Mrs. Brooks, I gather?" Saved by Ellen, and I breathe for the first time in what seems like ten minutes.

"Yes," my dad offers. "Thank you so much for taking care of our girl. What is your favorite flavor milkshake? I'll get you one from the shop across the road." Food's my dad's way of taking care of people. Seeing it from this hospital bed now, it makes sense.

He can't make his daughter eat, but he sure as hell offers it to those who will take it.

"That's so sweet of you, Mr. Brooks. I love their strawberry milkshakes! What a doll your dad is, Ms. Ruby!" She works on getting my blood pressure and heart rate. "Your blood pressure is up, girl! Yay! It's eighty-eight over fifty-five. Your body needed the fluids! We will monitor it until we are sure you are in the stable range. Your heart rate is up to forty-five beats per minute. That's so much better than the thirty-three you clocked in the ambulance!" She does not realize, but her words are tearing my dad to shreds.

"Her heartbeat was thirty-three during a run? Ruby, no." He shook his head in disbelief and sat in the visitor's chair as Patricia rubbed his back. Her left hand was strategically placed over her heart.

Thirty-three beats per minute…

"It's okay, Dad. It's only that low because I'm an athlete," I offer, but he snaps back immediately.

"Athlete? You think this is normal behavior for athletes? Athletes fuel their bodies, Ruby, not break them down!" His voice jumps, and he buries his head in his hands again and lets the air escape his lungs.

"What do you want me to say?" I yell, and I hate myself for it.

"The truth, Ruby, *the truth*. Do you even realize what you are doing?" He waits for an answer.

"Yes! I mean, no. God, Dad, how can I answer that question?" I'm flustered, and my heart monitor jumps.

"That's the problem, Ruby. You can't. You seriously can't because you haven't rehearsed your answer yet. It's easy to skirt around the truth when you are hundreds of miles away, but you can't lie to me to my face. You just can't." He's right. I feel my chest restrict even more than when I passed out, but it was different this time. I was watching my dad's heart break right in front of me, and it's pain caused solely by me and my stupid disorder.

"I'm sorry, Dad. I really am. I'll get help. I promise. I'll get better. I will." I see his face crumble, and I try to smile through the brokenness that I'm experiencing. "I've got it, Dad. I do. The Weston thing threw me off track, but I'm ready to do what it takes to get healthy. No more overdoing it." I say it so sincerely that I almost believe it. The truth is, ever since that night in the bathroom with Marco, I wasn't sure how to stop. It was a habit that turned into a problem that then became an entity out of my control.

I'm Frankenstein's monster.

"I hope you're right, Ruby Leigh. We can't lose you." His voice trailed as he looked out the window over the droll parking lot.

"I've got it, Dad. I will be okay. I'm not giving up." And I mean it.

"I trust you, Ruby. Please don't let me down," he begs.

"I promise, Dad. I'm going to get help."

"I know that you will." He smiles and wipes his last tear from his cheek. "I know you will. Listen, I have to go. I love you, Ruby Leigh. Remember, you'll always be my little girl." And he walked into the hallway to find the doctor.

I let the sobs escape as soon as his white sneakers disappeared around the corner. *I'm going to get help.* Avoiding feeling any type of pain is a luxury that no one can afford because to accomplish it, you have to sell your soul to the devil himself. My eating disorder is the wolf that I've been feeding, and the carnage that is now exposed can't be unseen.

There are three things I know for sure: Weston is gone for good, my dad will blame himself for my deterioration, and I will only stop running when I'm dead. Now to find Ellen. I'm getting out of here.

My wolves keep me company while I wait for her to return.

CHAPTER 11

Thursday, October 21, 2021

Today *feels* different.

The chill in the air feels permanent, and I put my hands in my pullover's pockets and rub my lap through the fuzzy fabric. The birds are quiet today, and I can hear the distant rumble of the custodian's cart on concrete. I lean my head back on the picnic table and stare at a cloud moving steadily through the sky like a leaf on the surface of a stream. I close my eyes and picture the rhododendrons bouncing in and out of the current on Sweetleaf. I wish I could put my feet in the water and feel the mist of the falls on my face.

I think about Cam. My heart contracts because it knows that it'll never be the same, but I'm becoming more and more okay with that. Michael's not the only one that crossed a line. I did too. I allowed myself to put my friendship with Cam before my marriage, and it almost cost me both. As women, we need female companionship, but when that connection surpasses boundaries, lines have to be redrawn. I think about when the lines began to blur, and it's clear looking back that

I was trying to save her from the pain that her divorce would bring. If I could be there for her, love her, support her, she'd be able to make it through. Somehow, she was me, seven and scared, and I couldn't let her drown. Although I'm sure having my support helped, I can't be so pompous to believe that she couldn't have done it without me. Cam is strong. She's gonna fight to protect her peace, and I'm thankful to have had a small part in helping her achieve that. She's done the same for me.

*****

Finally home from work, and I've got a minute to myself.

Thank you, Jesus.

I open the front door, expecting a mess, but to my surprise, it's pristine. It throws me off for a second because I'm used to immediately switching from teacher to maid, but this scene is unfamiliar and welcome. The sink is empty of dried cereal and the million drinking cups that accumulate in a mere twelve hours between the four of us, so I make myself a fresh cup of coffee and plop onto the island stool. Panda plunders his way down the hall, sounding the alarm that a treat is imminent, and he struggles to make it up to his destination on the high seat next to me. I give him a chin scratch, and he's happy. One of his favorite things about coffee is getting to lick the leftover froth in my mug. I've never had a friend that gets my anxiety around food, but I sure have an old disordered soul stuck in a fluffy cat's body who makes me feel a little less alone in my fight with my mind over food.

I love Panda for that.

I give him a pat and grab my mug. I'll regret this caffeine at ten o'clock, but I need the magic bean's power to even make it to then. I feel the weight of the porcelain in my weary hand, and I let the smooth hot liquid hit my lips with a sting. "Alexa, shuffle Ruby's Playlist."

"Shuffling Ruby's Playlist," Alexa responds, and I wait for her first choice. I hear the acoustic rip, and then Ben belts out, "*Annalee woke up every morning at the crack of dawn, to the screaming inside her head, and it was always worse than it ever was, and she could ruin things for everyone.*"

This is one of my favorite things to do when I'm home alone. With no one to serve, coach, teach, guide, or parent, I get to be *myself.* Each song that has made it to my playlist has significant meaning in one way or another with a memory connected to it: a heart break, an adventure, a moment of ecstasy—the list goes on. With every three-second pause between tracks there is an anticipation of which direction my emotions will soar next. It may sound brutal, but it's actually truly freeing. You see, in that moment in time when that particular song had meaning in my life, I was experiencing the good, the bad, and the ugly in real time, and it was traumatically wonderful. However, it was out of my control. Now, after all the work I did to evolve my thinking, it's nice to go back and reanalyze the situation in my right mind. Since I was deep in my eating disorder for so many primary years, I sometimes have a distorted view of an event or situation. Looking back on it now, I see the truth more clearly because I'm okay with who I am and how I have gotten here.

Take the first song Alexa threw at me: "Annalee." The whole song is about how this one woman is her own kryptonite. Whether it's her fault or not, her internal spiral is like the proverbial tornado that devastates the sleepy town. But the *volta* at the end of the song says it all: "But once you've seen her shine, you blink your eyes, how could you believe that you'd seen the hand of God." Yonder Mountain String

Band is brilliant, and this song shows it. They use a classic Shakespearian technique to truly pound in the point of "we're not perfect, but we are beautiful humans all looking for connection and love." It gets messy, but it's human nature and every human's right to pursue their peace.

It's my right.

The old me would have paid attention to the negative tone of the song. The whole beginning is basically calling this woman toxic and exposing her inner demons, but in the end, she is compared to the *hand of God.* That's what I'm choosing to focus on now. Yes, I'm a mess. Yes, I'm emotional. Yes, I'm broken. But you know what? I'm *worthy.*

I sip my coffee and smile. That's one thing I've noticed lately. I allow myself to smile and laugh. I don't wait for the appropriate moment or when others pave the way for an acceptable chuckle. Nope. I let smiles and laughs flow freely. Seems ironic, laughing when my world is crumbling, but maybe that is just it. I've been through so many setbacks in this life, yet here I am. As the saying goes, I have survived every bad day so far, so why would I not survive this? This kind of thinking is actual progress for me. I used to make myself sick thinking of all possible outcomes or the worst-case scenarios, but now, I could care less. Case in point: I'm sitting here drinking coffee and petting my disordered cat instead of giving up on life. Progress.

The old me would've made Michael's slipup about my not being enough somehow, but this time, I know that's *not the truth.* I'm worthy of a loyal, trustworthy, doting husband, and I'm surely going to demand it without feeling any guilt or shame. I'm not perfect, but *no one is.* Man it feels good to admit that, accept that, feel that. It truly is.

That also means I need to give Michael the same grace that I've wanted in the past, and I know that in my heart. Now to put that into action, that's another monster.

Alexa breaks the intrusive thought by starting the next track, and I hear the magical combination of piano and chimes while "Silver Springs" begins to fill the room. Great. The ultimate dreamy breakup song. Not a good omen, universe. Stevie Nicks belts out, "Was it worth it? Really, I don't want to know," and my mouth goes sour, so I put down my coffee. Figures my playlist would test me today. I was just all high and mighty one song prior, and now I'm a mess. See, just because you have conquered one trauma in your life doesn't mean that the others will dissipate. They require work too. Stevie's haunting voice is a reminder:

If I want a good marriage, it's gonna take work.

Confession: sometimes I try to cheat fate. "Alexa, next song!" and the symphonic lullaby of "Paradise" by Coldplay rings out. I slowly walked, heel to toe, to the center of the kitchen while Chris Martin sang out, "When she was just a girl, she expected the world, but it flew away from her reach, so she ran away in her sleep and dreamed of paradise every time she closed her eyes." Now this is a jam I can get into, so I begin to sway to the music surrounding me. "In the night, the stormy night, she closes her eyes." I close my eyes and let the darkness wash over me. "In the night, the stormy night, away she flies!"

I love storms.

My bare feet stick to the wood as I twist and turn to the vibrations that are echoing in my core. My arms are as fluid as the river flowing in the air above as my hips dip low to the earth. This is why I love listening to music alone. I feel free to fully feel the impact of the experience without judgment. I think maybe that is why I isolate in times like these, so I can be free to *feel*. I was so often stifled emotionally as a child that I never felt free to feel. But that's not the case any longer. Here in my kitchen, at thirty-seven years old, I'm free to *feel*. Maybe one day I will be free to feel when I'm not alone.

I open my eyes amid the last chorus, and the feeling of freedom to feel was suddenly lost because Panda and Murphie are looking at me as though I have lost all common sense. I giggle at their confusion and go to the fridge to get dinner started. "Wonderwall" by Oasis floods the room that's now suddenly covered with tiny rainbows from the crystal prism hanging in the kitchen window. Sounds cheesy, right? It is, but I love the rainbows that come twice daily. Once in the morning and once in the evening, the sun hits the back of the house just right and little rainbows fill the walls of our cozy home. It feels magical each time, like looking up at the stars in the black sky. It just never gets old seeing the universe show off.

I open the veggie drawer and grab a handful of items. I'm making my mom's broccoli and cheese soup tonight, and it makes me smile to think of her. She's been through it in her lifetime. As a boomer who soaked up every ounce of the stick-it-to-the-man movement of the '70s, she now works on saving the world one broken human at a time through her energy work in Brevard, and the things I used to tease her for are now commonplace in my household: crystals, sage, incense, and herbal tea. She's too kind to say, "I told you so," but I deserve it. I didn't give her enough credit for raising me back then, but I see how I got it wrong. My mom's never apologized for being human, and her enlightened sense of self came off as cold at times. I've recently come to the conclusion that she was not being cold but giving me a gift I can thank her for now as an adult. She taught me indirectly to protect my peace by modeling how she protected her own.

Although I blamed the divorce on her for so many years, I now see why she didn't settle. Everyone deserves respect alongside love, and I know my mom didn't want her daughters to witness her accept anything otherwise from a partner. Both she and my dad have expressed over the years that they should've handled their unraveling differently, but I stopped fantasizing about what my childhood could've been when I stepped out of Manna House. I believe it's best to trust the universe when it comes to all outcomes. No matter how unfair or how unjust, if we spend our lives on the "what ifs," we'll miss the beauty of the "here and now." My parents' divorce taught me one thing: the wolf you feed wins, and I refuse to feed the beast that's threatening my happiness. The wolves don't swarm because they get no food from me anymore. I've finally learned to feed myself, and as simple as it may sound, it's made my life worth living.

Thank you, Mom.

I get it now.

As if on cue, I hear the twang of the electric guitar, and my hero Tom Petty states from his chest, "Well, I won't back down. No, I won't back down. You can back me up to the gates of hell, but I won't back down. I won't back down," as the chorus belts, "Hey, baby, there ain't no easy way out. I will stand my ground, and I won't back down." This is a sign, and *I know it.* This is a tough time, *yes.* I'm hurt by Michael's actions, *of course.* I feel like I'm on the verge of using disordered behaviors, *absolutely,* but *I can't. I won't.*

I can't because I have come too far to give into the vices of my past.

I won't because I have goals and aspirations for my life that *don't* involve being disordered.

I have a core memory of a girl in college dancing for hours on end *so strangely* to a local band at the Dark Horse

Tavern. If there's any way to describe it, I would say that it was a cross between a cartoon villain dramatically sneaking across the screen with his hands and feet raised in unison with each step and the classic Nick Miller moonwalk away from a conversation in *New Girl*, but the freedom in her movement will forever stick in my mind. Anytime I need to get out of a funk, her dance always does the trick to snap me out of it. For the whole eight minutes and thirty-four seconds of the song, I danced and danced. I danced so intensely that my head began to hurt, and I stopped and let my head fall back, and my chin stretched toward the ceiling. I heard a knock. I was in full expressive dance mode smack-dab in the middle of the front porch windows, so I proceeded with caution, knowing that I may have been caught by whomever was on the other side of the door.

I was shocked when I opened it. There stood Michael holding flowers. "What are you doing knockin'? I thought you had a meeting in Atlanta?" I stood there embarrassed at the fact that, of course, it was *he* who witnessed me dancing.

He shook his head and smiled. "I was tryin' not to scare you by barging in while you were…you were…" He cracked a smile, and his chest filled with air, trying not to laugh.

"Dancing! I was dancing!" I hit him, grabbed the yellow roses out of his hands, and turned toward the kitchen.

"Is that what you call that?" He looked at me for permission, and I rolled my eyes and let out a giggle. He threw his head back in laughter, and I couldn't help but join in. Belly laughing is my favorite thing to do with Michael.

Well, my second favorite thing.

"Shut up. It's just something I do." I headed to the sink to trim the stems, and the smell of the flowers sent sensory tingles through my chest. I used to resent that Michael never bought me flowers. After years of wishing and wanting, I said *forget it* and started buying flowers for myself. Wouldn't you know, as soon as I started coming home with bouquets, the standard was set. That small act of fulfilling my own desires somehow gave me permission to continue the trend in all the other areas of my life. Suddenly, I didn't need Michael to treat me like a queen. I treated myself like the queen I am, and it made all the difference.

"What do you mean *it's something you do*?" He propped his foot up on the stool and leaned his elbow on the counter. I felt the energy shift instantly. I've missed his body's magnetic pull the past few days, and the tingles that started in my chest quickly traveled to my pelvic floor. The sudden and strong pulse of my anticipating vagina made me jerk, and I turned from him to try and save face, but it was too late.

I was caught.

I want him so badly.

He walks behind me at the sink, and he reaches around my waist to assist with trimming the stems, and the pressure of his body against my back is too much. I drop the flowers in the sink and turn around. His big hands slowly lift to cradle my chin and bring my mouth toward his. His chest is heaving, and I know that he's about to lose control from the wild look in his eyes. I always assumed that attraction faded over time, but I've discovered that our version of love is the opposite. He knows every curve of my body and yet *still* wants to explore it daily.

It wasn't always like this. The first few years of our marriage, I was so disordered that I *loathed* sex. After breaking up with Weston, I was terrified to open up to anyone else. Gone were the days of free-for-all. I hated the feeling of being vulnerable and exposed while also being expected to perform. It's impossible to enjoy physical connection when you're in that headspace.

Instead of honoring the place I was in with my body and mind, I put on an act, as many women do, and I merely offered my body to keep *him* happy. I didn't experience orgasms. I didn't look forward to being intimate. It was a duty that I fulfilled as a wife, and *it sucked*. After treatment, I quit feeling ashamed of this, and I opened up about it to Michael. I have to give him *so* much credit because instead of letting his ego get in the way, he embraced learning about me, my wants and my needs sexually, and the hard work paid off! He researched, he practiced, and we talked. Best decision ever made in our marriage because now, I can't wait to get him behind closed doors. Turns out, he is a *great* learner.

I allowed the weight of my head to rest in his grasp, and he put his lips to my forehead, to my cheek, and then to my lips, kissing them only partially, which is a *whole* other sensation. It gets me twitching again, and I press against him with vigor. He understands exactly what I'm offering, and he allows his hands to leave my face to embrace my waist as he pulls me onto him, prompting me to trust him with my body.

Trust.

That is hard.

But this feels so right.

I fully wrap my legs around him as he lifts me easily and slips his hands under my ass. He holds me as we press our foreheads together, and he stares deep into my eyes. I allow my lips to take over, and I kiss his cheek with a gentle force, and his grip tightens. I move to his neck, and it tastes like sweet sweat mixed with shaving cream, and I'm gone.

As my tongue is teasing his sensitive collar bone, he effortlessly charges us into the bedroom, and I've never wanted him more. My skin is crawling with anticipation, and he places me on the bed with the perfect amount of force. The playlist gods work their magic once more, and I hear the distinct drums and guitar picking begin. It's our song. Dierks Bentley's "Black" begins, and so does the best makeup sex of my life.

He is intensely staring in my eyes, and I can feel the energy radiating from his fingertips as he gently pulls my shirt over my head. My breasts are exposed, and he cradles them with his hands. I used to keep my body under wraps when I battled anorexia, but now, I long to be touched. He bows his head to my chest and takes in the beauty of my curves. My nipples are erect, and I can feel them ache for his obsessive attention. He feels my silent command, and he begins tonguing my nipple while lifting my breasts as if they were the most delicious fruit after the threat of a famine. A warmth radiates between my thighs, and my hands shoot to my hair to try to regain any control of my physical body, but I'm way past the point of no return. He moves slowly down my belly and lands his lips on my hip bones, and his fingers make their way down my panty line.

Yes, sir.

He makes his way to my core, and I'm flushed with heat. Recently, he has perfected the art of warming up my G-spot with his strong thick fingers, and the flicking motion right on my vaginal ridge makes my body beg for more. I used to think getting fingered was pointless, but after I healed my body issues, our sexual communication has helped both of us get exactly what we need to climax. He takes my sheet-gripping resistance as the go ahead sign, and he places his left palm on my pelvic bone and intensifies his concentration on my pleasure. I was on the verge of cumming but not willing to be finished yet. I pushed him off of me playfully with a scream, and now it's my turn to take control of the narrative. My entire body is buzzing in the best way possible, and there is nothing I want more than to feel him deep inside of me.

In one swift motion, I jump to my knees, place my palms firmly on his chest, and force his back to the bed. His lips are parted, and the intensity in his eyes is intoxicating. He approaches sex like a man on a mission, and I'm the one who benefits always! My tongue starts at his heaving chest and travels the familiar terrain. I swear, as the years go on, he only grows in size. It's amazing. I wrap my right hand around his shaft and seductively wet his member for maximum pleasure. I flick and twist my tongue to counteract the stroking of my hand. He grips the sheets next to his hips and then grabs my head with a groan of delight, and I pulse in anticipation for the main event.

Now it is his turn to be in control. He intently grabs my face and pulls it to his. I seductively make my way up onto his lap and slowly allow him to enter. His mouth rounds out into an oval expression of familiar ecstasy, and my head falls back, and my chin drops as if I'm a wolf howling at the moon. I let out a faint gasp of satisfaction, and I began to work my thighs slowly up and down, allowing the wetness to saturate him. I hold myself up by pushing him down, but all his fight is gone. He lays back with his eyes wide and focused on mine. His hands make sure to embrace every inch of my exposed chest, stomach, and legs. He reaches back to firmly grab my ass, and he is done. He has reached his peak, and now it is time for me to join in for the final scene.

He throws me off of him to the side, flips me on my stomach, and I reach for the pillow in desperation for support. I look back at him as he wets his palm to help entry, but he has me so wet that it's not needed. I feel his dick break through my tightness, and the tip beautifully pounds that warmed up G-spot. He rhythmically thrusts over and over again, and I grip the sheets so hard that I rip them off the mattress.

He knows without me asking, and he doesn't hesitate.

Harder and harder, he thrusts, and goose bumps form from my cheeks to my toes. I close my eyes as the orgasm builds and then let out a scream of pleasure when his final drive makes me see stars. I'm in a full-body erotica, and I feel him release into me as he lets out a grunt and spasms with me in unison.

My world is now black in the best way possible.

He lingers until both of our body quakes subside, and he rolls over on his back with his hand steady on the small of my back. I'm mush, melted into the sheets, breathing heavily into the cocoon my folded arms have made. I lift my head, turn to the right, and meet eyes with my skilled lover.

"Man, Big Mama, that was amazing." He put his hands behind his head and turned to catch my eye. "I felt your goose bumps. They were all over. It's so fucking sexy to get you off." He closed his eyes in a proud smile.

"You're good at it." I pause as insecurity begins to wash over me, and I flip over and cover up with the sheet. "That's why the proposition to Cam just seemed out of nowhere. I mean, I know we have our issues, but sex has not been one of them since I've been recovered."

"It truly has nothing to do with sex, Rubes. That's obvious. It's just… I depend on you for everything: friendship, intimacy, companionship, adventure, and when you started getting close to Camryn a few years ago, it felt like she was taking my place. You no longer needed me for all the things. You had Cam. You no longer needed my opinions or insights. You had Cam. You no longer wished for weekends away with me. You wanted to escape with Cam. I've been frantically trying to figure out how to get back to it being us, and my dumbass landed on inviting her in bed. What a fucking idiot."

In all fairness, this truly makes sense. I've only had one other female friend in my life since meeting Michael, and Joanna's always lived two states away. Looking back, when she would visit, Michael would always act possessive. He would get nervous, call me a ton to check in when we were out, and he always made a point to be extraphysical with me when she was present. Now looking back, I see the similar patterns. He once crashed our girls' night in Athens because he said I didn't respond to his text as quickly as normal, so he thought something was wrong. The little incidents that played like a movie in my mind were overwhelming, and it made my head spin.

"Dammit, Michael! What you did was messed up. You know that, right?" I looked up at him as tears overflowed my lids. He wiped them off my cheeks as he then worked on his own.

"I know, babe. I have some deep rooted issues that I really need to figure out, and I plan to. I just want you to know how sorry I'm that my insecurities have now ruined your friendship with Cam. You don't deserve that, and neither does she." He lets his chin fall to his chest, and I lift it so his eyes are square with mine.

"I want you to hear me on this. I know that we've been through hell together, and I know that my disorder painted us into an isolating corner at times in our marriage, but I love you, and I'm not going anywhere. In sickness and in health, you are my husband. I don't want anyone else—just you, love. I just want you."

With those words, he crumbled into my arms. I held him and let him sob on my bare shoulder. I could feel his tears pooling on my collarbone then racing down my chest before landing abruptly on the sheets. I held him tightly, the same way he held me many breakdowns before. It is a beautiful thing when the truth comes out because what is left is a clean and pure hole that is ready to be filled with all the good now that the ugly has been evicted.

I waited until I felt his breathing go to a normal pace, and then I pulled back to look him in the eyes. "Michael, I'll never leave you. You're my *soul mate*. You are my *person*. You are my *future*. We need to address these feelings of not enough because that's so far from the truth that it isn't funny."

He shakes his head and pulls me into the biggest hug of my life. I allow myself to sink into his embrace, and as always, it makes me feel safe. I close my eyes and squeeze my arms as hard as I can around his neck. Our bodies again are pressed against one another without any barriers, and his hands run up and down my back with just the right amount of pressure. Alexa, as if on cue, begins to play David Gray's song "This Year's Love," and we both pull back and smile.

"Dance with me, beautiful?" All the sudden, he is out of the bed, and in all of his naked glory, he is prompting me to the wooden floors with his head bowed and his arm extended.

"You are crazy!" I place my hand in his anyway.

It was one of those times in life when words would only take away from the beauty of the moment, so we were silent. The sound of the piano flooded the room, and we swayed in the afternoon sun to the haunting lyrics. "This year's love, it better last. Heaven knows it's high time. I've been waiting on my own for too long." My head rested on his bare chest, and his hand was firmly placed in the small of my back. Our bodies swayed as one, proving as always to me that sex was not the only way that we connect deeply.

As the song came to an end, so did our dance. He put his thumb under my chin, lifted my face to his, and spoke into my lips, "You're my world, Ruby Blue."

"And you're mine," I replied.

I knew that this conversation was far from over, but we both needed to let this sink in. One thing that this situation has taught me is that patience is a gift that you give the ones you love because without it, you are not honoring their experience in this life, and you can't force anything that is not meant to be. Michael and I are meant to be. I have known it since the day he stepped foot in my classroom. He is my husband, my person.

I will fight for him like he has fought for me.

*****

Michael offered to pick up the kids, so I'm left alone, naked in the afternoon sun, and suddenly, I see it: the full-size gold mirror that still has been hiding its truth under the safety of a throw blanket that I tossed over it not even a week ago.

Do it.

I stare at it with a renewed confidence brought on by holding boundaries and great sex.

Take it off.

My naked body begs to be exposed in all its rawest form.

All it takes is thirty seconds of courage.

I remember a sermon that stated, "All it takes to do something brave is thirty seconds of courage." I used this simple prompt when I was scared to try something new or complete a difficult meal at Manna House many times, and admittedly, it works.

It's time to see the truth.

I grab a corner of the blanket with my thumb and forefinger, and I give it a slight tug as if it's Urim and Thummim and will make the choice for me. It slips slowly at first, caught by the resistance of the corner, but gravity can't cease to exist because of insecurities. It stacks like an accordion at the base, and I allow my eyes a pause before I look.

Practice what you preach, Rube.

I allow my gaze to travel from my teal-painted toes to my well-worn shins. I travel the scar where they harvested my vein to replace the artery in my arm, and I count the staple tracks as I go: twenty-seven.

I take in my legs. I think of how they've changed over the years. Once they were made of discovery and joy, and they created an adventure out of creeks and crawdads. Once they were pure mission and muscle that carried me miles and miles and miles from my mind. Then they were merely bone, afraid and fractured, waiting for nightfall so there was a hope of happiness in dreams. And now they are a combination of all of the above, and my daytime is no longer a nightmare, and my dreams only make me ready to be awake. That's how it should be. I don't pretend to understand the inner workings of God and the universe, but I do know they never intended legs to be idolized for their *looks*. I want to get back to my legs being created for adventure, not display.

I scan my eyes to my belly, and I touch its softness with a compassion I've never experienced before. I'm beginning to get a bit of rippling in my lower abdomen, and I let my fingers brush the tiny shadows of the crevasse as I think of how beautifully silky it feels. I used to pride myself in my defined abs and flat belly, but this feels more authentic. This belly has helped create life. Who actually cares if it looks like it did when I was sixteen?

I cradle my newly formed breasts, and their weight in my hands gets my heart racing, and I feel grateful that when I regained weight after treatment, my body blessed me with boobs. The best part about them is not their size but their sensitivity. I get the hype now.

I place my hands around my throat and lift my chin to feel its length. I cross my hands and let them slip down the opposite arm when I finally turn to meet my own gaze. My eyes are sky blue, and I can tell I've been worked up by the brightness of their center. I touch the soft lines that fan out from their corners, and I smile to make them full-on crow's-feet, and I stroke my cheek in approval.

Am I society's version of beautiful? I'm trying to get to the point that I don't care. Am I my own version of beautiful? I think so. Why? Because I'd rather believe I'm made of the same material as the stars than believe what a cooperation that profits off my insecurities sells me.

Yes, I'm made of stardust, mountain runoff, and Prometheus's fire.

I'd much rather shine than shrink.

CHAPTER 12

Monday, February 22, 2016

"Mama!" Hudson yells from the training potty in the hall bathroom.

"Hold on, buddy. I'm getting Nali changed!" I frantically wiped the sticky poop off her raw butt cheeks. Her skin is so sensitive, and her poor bum's raw.

"Ouchy! It hurt, Mama!" Her raspy two-year-old voice breaks my heart.

"I know, baby. I know. I'll get the cream. I'm sorry." She lets the whimpers push through her closed lips, and her chin quivers in pain.

"Maaaamaaaaa!"

"I'm coming, Hud. Give me a minute!" I wrestle Nali's swift kicks of protest.

"Mama." Uh-oh, a tone shift. Shit.

I fasten a new diaper on Nali and sprint to Hudson to see the damage. "Sorry, bud, I was…" The smell hits my nostrils with a vengeance.

Oh.

My.

God.

"I tried to wipe." Hudson dropped his head in shame, and his hands and bum were smeared with a brown paste that was not chocolate.

"Oh, buddy, good try." My gag reflex is nonexistent due to my constant purging, and for once, it works in my favor. I begin to work on his hands first, and there's no way the one towel I have will take care of it. "Hold on, son."

"Okay, Mama. I'm sorry."

"It's fine, Hud. Don't touch anything." I ran back to my bedroom where I left Nali. When I round the corner of the master bath, I see a plume of powder slowly floating to the ugly linoleum.

"Look, Mama, snow!" Nali is sitting cross legged on the floor, and her entire body is covered in baby powder. She proudly slams the open container's bottom against the ground, and I feel as though I'm watching LeBron James's home court intro, and I stand dumbfounded as the room is covered in white once again.

"What the—" I stop myself. She's repeating everything these days. "Nali, we just got out of the bath." She swirls her tiny fingers in the mess. She circles them around her little legs and never unlocks her eyes from mine.

"Mama!" Crap. I forgot about Hud. I race back to the hall bath, and he's taken it upon himself to use the shower curtain to help the cleaning process, and he smiles proudly. "I'm all clean now!" I look at what used to be a bathroom. There's shit all over the floor, the curtain, and the sink. Hud's butt is caked, and he's running his finger up and down his thigh, trying to feel out my reaction before he commits to his approach. He just turned four last week, and although he's been potty-trained for two years, pooping is still a work in progress.

"Don't touch anything else, Hud. Walk with me." The smell hits me harder this time, and I hold back a retch. He holds up his hand for guidance since his undies are impeding his stride, and I take it reluctantly.

"Where we goin'?

"To the bath." I taste bile coming up.

"We just took a bath!"

"Well, bud, we've got to get this poop off you somehow!"

We shuffled into the master bath, and when we turned the corner, Hud was elated. "Elsa came. Elsa came!" He broke loose of my grip, tried to run, tripped on his whitey tighties, and fell face-first in a pile of powder. He placed both hands slowly on the ground with authority. I've learned the longer the pause, the louder the release, so I cringed and waited for the wail. The scream pierced my soul, and Nali joined in the howl like a loyal pack member, and I wished the wolves would come take me now.

In times like this, the world seems to happen in three words or less so as not to confuse importance: check Hud first. No blood. Good. Turn on water. Make it warm. Add bubbles for enticement. Lots. Over amount. The whole bottle. Hud, in the tub. Nali, in the tub. Screams continue. I might lose it. Phone rings. It's Michael. Text: "Gonna be around 11 PM, game running behind." Fuck. *Fuck.* I need to get away. I need to run. More screams. Can't take the screams. Toilet. I need the toilet. Get me out of here. If I hear, "Mama," one more time...

"Maaaaammmmmaaaaa!"

"Shuuuuuttttt uppppp!

Silence.

Their eyes were wide with fear and lips quivering in shock. I can't take it. I dove into the quarter bath and slammed the door. I could hear their whimpers, and a pain in my chest forced my face to grimace, and I covered my ears to try and escape.

The downside of silence is that it gives my eating disorder the mic. It's like my brain sets up a podium, and out emerges this demanding demon that dictates the direction of my thoughts. I listen because its commands are deafening. I follow because I want it to stop. I give in because I want the urge to be satisfied. I let it out to cleanse my body. I fall prey because I'm defenseless. I'll even take the chaos over the demands. I can't think. My eyes search for reason. There's none to be found. This is my life. This is my brain. What am I doing? I need it out of me. I want it gone.

I shove my fingers down my throat. The smell of shit leftover hits my nose, and I remember the reason why I have a second with the toilet alone. I'm both disgusted and grateful. The smell really made puking a breeze, and I retched until there was nothing left in me. As if to punish me for being such a sicko, my stomach continued to dry heave over and over and over long after it was emptied. My eyes felt as though they would pop out of their sockets, and my ears were ringing with a vengeance. The high-pitched ring was just low enough for me to hear the whimpers of my confused children, scared in the tub.

"What is wrong with you?" I scolded myself. My head was spinning, my arms crossed on the toilet and my head dangling in the bowl. I banged my fist on the seat and the clank of the cracking porcelain made Nali scream. I heard Hud say, "It's okay, Nali. It's okay." I let out a sob that came from deep within.

"Mama, you okay?" Hudson asked.

"Mama?" Nali joined in.

I rubbed my thumb over the sharp edge of the broken seat. I pushed my flesh harder against the jagged porcelain waiting to hear the skin give way. There's a rip and a pain that sends a wave of relief over my body, and for a split second, the world floats on around me, but I'm now the grounded one. I'm shaken prematurely from my high by banging on the door behind me. I see Hud's toes wiggling under the door, and then his fingers join. I hold my blood dripping hand to my chest and bite my lip for stability. My face is a wreck. "I'll be out in a sec, Bud." I manage, but I feel a throbbing in my lip. I taste metal and touch the wound for proof. Blood is dripping from my chin, and I examine it with my good hand. How did I get here? How did I allow it to get to this? I'm disgusting. Everyone would be better without me. I fantasize about Michael finding comfort in his colleague, the girls' varsity assistant coach, whose gaze lingers on his tight khakis a little too long when he walks by.

He'd be better off with her.

"Mama, I cold," I hear Nali plead.

"Coming, love. Hold on." I wipe my face in my shirt and wrap the sleeve of it around my hand. I attempt to open the door, but I have to wait for Hudson to move his bare feet screeching as he slides them slowly across the floor, mocking the irony of my life at the moment. I'm trapped by my ED, and it only allows me to come to join the land of the living for one purpose: to parent. And if I'm honest, I'm barely doing that.

"Hey, Mama. You okay?" Hudson's brows are knit together, and his horse-soft forehead is crinkled in concern.

I unsuccessfully attempt to hide my wounds, but this is the kid who notices if the shadows on the moon are different. There's no fooling him. "Yeah, bud. I just slipped and bit my lip. I'm okay."

"You broke the seat."

"Yeah, I did when I fell. But it's okay. Daddy'll fix it."

"Daddy's gonna be mad?"

I think about what I'm going to tell Michael. He no longer believes a word that comes out of my mouth, and I can't blame him.

"No, Hud bud, he'll just be glad I'm okay. Let's get your sister." I stand up and wipe a tear discreetly, but Nali sees me.

"You cryin', Mama?" I bend down to wrap her in the towel Mimi got her with the mermaid hood, and I hugged her a bit too tight.

"No, love, no. Just bit my lip, see?" I let her examine my wound.

"You can't eat lips, silly!" She giggled at her joke, and it hurt when I smiled.

"Oh, man, I forgot! Next time, remind me not to!" I kiss her forehead, and I leave a drop of blood on her pristinely fair skin. The stain sat there, staring at me, blaming me. It's there as a sign, as a brand, as a scarlet letter. It seems to be a stamp that solidifies the download is complete: generational eating disorder. Check. I take the dirty powder-covered washcloth off the floor and attack the stain like her life depended on it.

"Ouch, Mama!" Her hands shot up in self-preservation, but she was no match for an ED-faced mama with guilt to get rid of.

"Time for bed." I whip Nali up in one arm and grab Hud's hand with the other.

"We need to brush, Mama." Hudson's confused.

"Two baths is enough." The pain in my chest is growing.

"I like two baths!" Nali exclaimed, her little hands clasping around my face.

"I'm so glad. Now, no stories tonight. Hop in bed."

"Can Nali sleep with me?"

"Yes. Do you want that Nali?"

"Yeah!" Her face is overcome with joy.

"Get your tag blankie." She almost leapt from my arms to comply.

As I'm turning down the covers, I look at my arms. They're bones. As I walk around the bed to the other side, I see my legs. They're skeletal. I lift up my sagging boxers and see Hud staring at me.

"Are you sick, Mama?" His eyes are pleading.

"Yeah, Hud, I am. But I'm going to be okay."

"You need to see a doctor?"

"Probably."

"Need me to hold your hand?"

"No, bud, that's not your job. You're my kid. I hold your hand."

"Mamas need their hand held too sometimes."

My throat constricts. I look at the ceiling to gain control.

"You're right, Hud. They do."

"I ready!" Nali had put her nightgown on backward, but I didn't fix it. She wiggled her way up the bed that's taller than her, and she nestled in right next to Hudson. He rolled his eyes as she closed hers. This dynamic is familiar. I pictured Charleigh letting me slip into bed next to her after I begged and begged.

"I love you both so, so much." I kiss their silky foreheads, and I feel the soreness of the self-inflicted hole in my lip. "Sweet dreams." I run my fingers through their hair and feel a wave of relief come over me as my parenting duties are done for the moment, but the second wave of guilt overpowers it. Panda heaves himself up on the bed and joins the party as if to make me feel better for leaving them. I hear their whispers over the white noise of the fan once the door closes, and I lean against it because my knees suddenly feel weak. I'm covered in baby powder, poop, and I smell like a cocktail of shit and vomit. I sink to the floor and wrap my arms around my knees. I pull my bones close, and I feel them ache with pressure from the ground. My chest heaves, and I cover my mouth to stifle the sob.

My eating disorder has the mic again, and it's poison washes over me. *You're a burden. You're sick. You're worthless. You're fat. You can't even be an anorexic properly. You have to puke because you're a failure, an eating disorder failure. You're not even skinny. You do all this for nothing. Fat cow, you fucking fat cow. No wonder Michael stays away. Who'd want to be near you? This is the beginning of the end. Everyone will leave you. Everyone will leave. You may as well give up. Hudson knows. He knows. He's gonna follow your lead. And Nali, forget her ever being confident. She'll be on the floor next to you one day. You're a waste, a fucking waste.*

My face is crumpled in my shaking hands. How did I get here? How did I let it get this bad? My mind replays the familiar guilt reel: divorce sets the scene, toxic love fills in the cracks, fleeing to Mississippi where no one knows me, almost running myself to death, fingers in my throat, face in the toilet, starving, starving, starving.

I can't stop.

Why can't I just stop?

I no longer hear the wolves in the shadows. I put a fucking collar and leash on one and named it Frank.

*****

By the time Michael gets home, it's close to midnight. I'd cleaned up the powder mess, cleaned the guest bath, and took care of the evidence of my quarter-bath episode, so he was oblivious to the fray that ensued only mere hours earlier. I'm usually resentful of his lack of understanding of how hard it really is to parent two kids under four solo, but tonight, I'm grateful for his absence and ignorance.

"Hey, Rubes, how was your day? He places his watch, whistle, and keys in the bedside table and begins to peel the layers off his body. He smelled of high school gym and Axe deodorant, but he still looked fresh at the end of his eighteen-hour day. I wish I could say the same.

"It was okay. Got hairy at the end, but we made it to bedtime alive."

Barely.

"Hate I missed seeing the kids again today. How was Nali's diaper rash?"

"Still terrible. She may be the next LeBron James, though." Michael slips off his trainers and roughly jumps in the covers. Although I tease him for being such an ogre, it's often his immature and playful nature that can shake me out of my own head.

"Well, she didn't get her ballin' skills from you. That's for sure!"

"Fair."

"You okay? I'm surprised you're still up."

"Yeah, I'm all right," I lied. "Just a long day."

"Need me to help put you to sleep?" Sex is the last thing I want right now.

"You know me so well," I lied again.

"Well come on over here!" He lifts the blankets to allow easy access, and his shorts come off immediately. He pushes himself against me and works his member between my frail legs. I wince in pain as he allows his weight to sink into me. His hands travel the length of my skeleton, and my skin feels taut against his touch. He's used to my bones protruding, but I still can't get used to his touch. I feel the tears begin to build, and I quickly flip over so he can finish, and I can cry without making him feel bad. I fake an orgasm when he climaxes, and he flips over on his back with a smile of satisfaction on his lips.

"That was great, Rubes. Thanks. I needed that."

"Me too."

"How'd you eat today? Did you run? Any slipups?"

"I ate, and I ran after school before I got the kids." At least one truth.

"How far did you go?"

"Three miles."

It was actually eight.

"And you ran this morning too, right?"

"Yeah, but only two miles, so five in total today."

Five in the morning and eight in the afternoon to be exact. Five sounds better than thirteen.

"Good! Glad you are listening to Dr. Sapphire and cutting back." He rolls over in the bed and adds, "If you stick with the meal plan, hopefully we can get your vitals stable and avoid any more hospital trips."

He's referring to the New Year's Day incident. We were at Papa's house celebrating with family, and food and drink were abundant. I ate all the things, drank all the things, puked all the things, and then passed out in the middle of Charleigh's beautifully constructed charcuterie board. It turns out that my potassium levels were dangerously low from the constant vomiting, so they kept me in the ER overnight for observations. I lied again and again to reassure the doctors that my eating disorder was in my past, but I left that day, stopped at Steak 'n Shake on the way home, ate a large Oreo milkshake, and puked in the downstairs bath before going up to kiss the kiddos good morning.

I'm getting reckless.

"No more hospital trips." I reassure him as I pull my nighttime panties up over my sore pelvic bones.

"Good night, Rubes."

"Good night."

"These violent delights have violent ends" (Shakespeare).

*****

I have an odd talent that most likely stems from over-thinking and hyper-self-awareness: I can actively participate in my dreams. Sometimes it's exciting, like I get to choose my own ending to the movie that's not going the way I want it to. Other times, it's terrifying because when I can't get control of my brain's narrative, I'm back at the mercy of the wolves, and the feeling of helplessness saturates my soul even as it sleeps. Tonight's nightmare is no surprise, and I feel as though I'm falling, falling, falling. The air is thin, the clouds are abundant, and there's no horizon in sight. In my subconsciousness, I know it's one of those dreams that I'll wake up right before I crash to the ground, but for the first time, I can't make out anything other than endless sky. I was in a free fall, tumbling end over end, arms flailing, mouth screaming, but nothing came out but a whisper.

Help.

As I'm falling, I see the darkness getting closer and closer. I desperately try to wake myself up, but my efforts are thwarted by fate. I'm plunging through space and time, and a great sadness washes over me like the clouds I'm plummeting through uncontrollably. The air whips my thinning hair, and my limbs thrash for anything to grasp, but there's only the vast nothingness that's become my existence.

Maybe I should give up.

Maybe I should give in.

Maybe I should let myself fall.

All of a sudden, my body's snatched from the atmosphere with a force that jolts me awake, and it feels like God himself just ripped me from the sky. I sit up in bed with a scream, and I feel my heart restart with the abrupt arousal. The clock reads 2:22 a.m., and without waking up, Michael rolls over next to me with deep breath escaping his chest. As I attempt to catch my breath, I can feel my heart struggling to keep up with its duty. This type of episode has happened before, and I know what I need to do. I stumble out of bed and begin doing jumping jacks with the intention of kick-starting my heart, but the blood rushes to my head, and I fall for real this time.

When I open my eyes, Michael is standing over me, begging me to wake up. His big hands cup my frail face, and I feel a sting above my right eye, and I reach for the spot that's throbbing with pain. My eyes adjust to the dim lamp that illuminates the room just enough, and I blink back into consciousness. "What happened?" I ask, but I'm putting the pieces together without assistance.

"You passed out again, Rubes. You were out for a while. You scared the shit out of me." I glance at the clock, and it reads 2:35 a.m.. I was out for thirteen minutes? Damn. That's a record.

"Yeah, I had a bad dream and stood up too fast." It's not exactly a lie.

"We can't do this anymore, Rubes. You're killing yourself! I'm calling Dr. Sapphire in the morning. I can't wake up to you dead, Rubes. I just can't." His lips are pursed together in a vain attempt to keep his cool, but I know he's close to calling it quits.

I don't know how to stop.

"I'm not dying," I state, but even my words seem pathetic to me.

"Yes, you are, Ruby. You are. And I can't watch the slo-mo train wreck anymore. Neither can Hudson and Nali. I refuse to let them watch you kill yourself. We're going to Manna tomorrow."

"I have to go to work, Michael. I can't just flake out on my responsibilities," I protest.

"You're gonna be dead in a month, Rubes! Your damn heart is giving out!"

"I just stood up too fast."

"Keep telling yourself that, Ruby, until the day you'll never stand again."

"I can't do it, Michael. I can't leave the kids." I think about Dr. Sapphire's statement last visit: "*It's forty-five days now in exchange for forty-five years of freedom from the chains of your disorder.*"

Maybe I like chains. Chains are limiting, but they're predictable. My ED's predictable. Its ebb and flow serves my anxious soul, and the aftermath is easy to overlook when the euphoria it summons feeds the wolves that threaten my peace.

"You're going tomorrow."

Make me.

CHAPTER 13

Wednesday, March 2, 2016

I lie awake staring at the ceiling in the cool dark morning. I feel as though I may float away with the lack of Murphie and Panda weight on top of my chest, and I regret not bringing a weighted blanket to Manna House like Dr. Sapphire suggested. The light from the hallway cascades across the spotless floor, and I see Dillon curled up in a ball in the twin bed next to me. She's my roommate. I've never shared a room with anyone besides Michael, so it's been interesting to say the least. One thing I've learned about eating disorder treatment, you're *never* alone. Dillon's from South Carolina, and she's a spitfire—nineteen, beautiful, athletic, and severely broken like everyone else in this house. There's sixteen of us in this last chance state, and I'm not sure what's worse, fighting my wolves or watching fifteen others in the thick of their own battle to the death. Sad part is, I watched one girl lose the first day I was here. She's now in the hospital on suicide watch.

This disease will try and kill you one way or another.

Dillon rolls over to face me with a sigh, eyes still shut in deep sleep, and I turn to the wall to feel a smidge of dignity.

Mornings are the hardest time of day for me. My body's so used to getting up at four o'clock to run that I've developed restless leg syndrome now that I'm forced to be stagnant 24-7. It starts at my toes and travels up to my hips. There's an empty ache that begs to be beaten out by concrete, and my body's so confused as to why I'm laid up in this bed instead of giving into its demands. I can't even do jumping jacks to substitute the negative energy buzzing through my veins. Falisha, the night nurse, caught me on the second night, and she now posts up right outside our door to listen for bare feet to touch ground. I swear, she's got dog-ears. I can't even get away with doing crunches under the covers. I guess I'm proving why constant supervision is necessary.

I look at the clock: 4:25 a.m., and the second hand ticking mocks my pathetic existence with its ability to control my day so strictly. My brain attempts to find comfort in the routine that I'm now a week into:

- Weigh-ins at 6:00 a.m. and then showers
- Breakfast promptly at 7:00 a.m.
- DBT class at 8:00 a.m.
- Snack at 9:00 a.m.
- Food chemistry with the dietitian Ann at 10:00 a.m.
- Body love at 11:00 a.m.
- Lunch at 12:00 p.m.
- Rest time is 1:00 to 2:00 p.m.
- Snack at 3:00 p.m.
- Mindful yoga at 4:00
- Phone time from 5:00 to 6:00 p.m.
- Dinner at 6:30 p.m.
- Free time from 7:30 to 9:00 p.m.

- Dessert at 9:00 p.m.
- Lights out at 9:30 p.m.

If I'm honest, the routine doesn't bother me. It actually has been the one comforting thing in this hellacious scenario. I've always been one to crave order, and through these therapy sessions, I'm learning why. My life was chaotic after the divorce. My dad moved from house to house for years, sleeping on people's couches, refusing to accept his and my mom's fate. While he was couch hopping, my mom was jet setting. She and Tim were in a whirlwind romance, and I was left living out of a suitcase most of the time, bouncing from couch to couch with Dad or being pawned off on a friend for the night or weekend by my mom. Their lies flowed like water, and the helplessness I experienced on a minute-by-minute basis turned me into a walking zombie. The light went out of my eyes after they divorced. I still hate looking at myself in pictures from that time. I see the wolf curled up sleeping in the corner of the sterile room. He opens one eye as if telling me he hears my thoughts, and he closes it slowly and is asleep once more.

Pet therapy's on Friday, Frank.

Eating is actually not as bad as I thought it would be. I was constipated for the first week, but another resident taught me a trick. If you put your heels up on the toilet seat in front of you, it lets things flow freely. For once in my life, someone is giving me permission to consume and enjoy food. And on top of that, I'm learning so much about the science beyond our bodies and their use and need for nutrients. Food chemistry with Ann is my favorite. She's a dietitian who loves animals and once struggled with a running addiction herself, so she understands the inner workings of my twisted mind. I also have found DBT helpful. Dialectical behavior therapy is the full name, but it's actionable tools that one can use to face a fear, work through anxiety. My two favorites I've learned so far are *fact-checking* and *opposite action*. Fact-checking allows me to separate the truth from my eating disorder's lies, and opposite action gives me the double-dog dare that's needed for me to push past the fears of going against everything I ever thought was truth connected with consuming food and maintaining a healthy body.

I hear footsteps in the hall, and my door opens slowly, and the light puts a golden wedge in the dark room. Falisha makes the most annoying *psst* sound that triggers a memory of a girl who sat behind me in multiple classes in college who was forever *psst*-ing me.

"Mama Rube, you wanna head start on showerin' this mornin'? I knows you up wit your runnin' lovin' ass. Come on. Us mamas need a break from dem kids."

Falisha gets me.

I mouth, *Thank you*, as I peel the covers off and feel the sedentary sting as my feet hit the hard floor. I grab my towel off the door and follow Falisha to the locked closet, where all our shower caddies are kept.

Sharp items are a hard no.

"Now don't go clogging up my drain with all that hair of yours. If I have to snake that shower one mo', time I'm gonna quit." She hands me my bin, and the smell of Dove reminds me of home.

"I'm trying to keep every strand, believe me."

Hair loss: major side effect of malnutrition. Falisha snakes a lot of drains around here.

"Well, git with it." And she takes her chair and sits next to the shower as I undress and slip through the clear-glass door. You'd think they'd put opaque doors since you're showering with four of your friends and Falisha, but nope. Everyone gets to see me shave my hoo-ha.

I don't really mind it, though. I've had a mind shift since coming to Manna House. In the body love group the other day, a girl said, "My body is the least interesting thing about me," and the statement made goose bumps rise all over my body. In one sentence, she gave a factual truth that broke the chains I bore for so long at my own doing, alongside a saturation of society's sick propaganda created to convince you that you're deficient. I'm not deficient. I'm just a soul that's chosen this path on earth, and with faith and purpose, I know I can make something beautiful from this shitstorm that's my life right now.

I'm learning that I can love storms without being one.

I do love storms.

But I love peace more.

"Mama Rube, git you're bin, hon. 'Bout to wake up the troupes."

I turn off the shower, grab my towel off the hook, and wrap it around my waist, and I try to ignore the noticeable change in my weight. It's hard to explain, but the body heals faster than the brain, and although I know the way I want to look at myself, it's gonna take time. I bend to clean all the hair out of the drain, and to my surprise, there's only a few strands.

And no wolf hair today.

As seven o'clock creeps closer, I check on Dillon to make sure she's on track to make it. She's in midcontour, and all the eyeshadow choices are fanned across the towel in front of the mirror. She's not only late but holding up everyone else.

"This is treatment, Dillon, not an event. You'll cry that off ten minutes into DBT. Come on. Need me to help you clean up? It's five to seven," I warn.

"Chill, Mama Rube. Life's the event! Isn't that what we're learning here?" The others moan and maneuver around her mess.

"We just can't be late one more time. Emily said there'd be a consequence."

"All right, teacher's pet. That's an oxymoron, right?"

"More like antithesis and irony, but not the point. Get your tail in the foyer before seven!"

"Damn, Mama, it's not that serious."

I heard Emily and Falisha discussing the consequence that will be our fate if any one of us is late again.

It's that serious to me.

"One minute, ladies!" Emily called, and I made my way to the others who were already starting down the stairs.

Complaints begin to circulate, and the energy shift is tangible.

"Come on, Dillon," someone yells up. "I ain't doing no consequence 'cause yo' ass late again!"

"Seven o'clock, ladies." Emily asks even though she damn well knows the answer, "Are we all accounted for?" Fifteen sets of eyes roll almost simultaneously. "Oh, boy. Missing one again, huh? Well, that stinks because your friend's inability to keep a schedule, breakfast plans have now changed."

Change, plans, and *food* are the three words that can suck the life right out of the room here at Manna, and they use them often as a way to get us ready for the real world that's not so kind to those in recovery. I know I need it, but it still blows.

"You will no longer be plating your waffles, bacon, and grits this morning. They will be portioned, plated, and placed in front of you."

My stomach flips. Plating my own food is essential for avoiding a panic attack, and that's the main reason I picked this hellhole over the other treatment centers. To someone who's not disordered, the action of food being picked, plated, and passed out is a dream. For someone who suffers from an eating disorder, it feels like the snake telling Eve, "It'll be fine. Just take a bite."

Wolves come in many forms.

"Go ahead and sit down. It'll be two minutes." Emily walks to the kitchen and gets in the assembly line to speed up plating. I cringe as I see them slop on the grits and let them seep into the waffle. They carelessly fork the first bacon that their jab produces, and it's as limp as an overdone noodle. My teeth begin to chatter, and I sit staring at the window as my familiar foe approaches the yard with a hunger in his eyes, expecting to be fed.

Emily begins placing the meal in front of the anxious and annoyed girls one by one. She gets to me, and I feel the urge to run. If I go now, I can make it to the gas station down the road before anyone could catch me, I thought, but before I could ditch, the plate's sat in front me, and the throbbing in my head pounds harder than my feet on asphalt. I see the greasy, soggy bacon that is one hundred percent underdone, and the grits have made the waffle inedible. I look anywhere but at the table, and my eyes land on a wallflower named Lily. She's a cross between Scarlett Johansson and Stevie Nicks, and she was born a burden to her mother. Thank goodness her dad's a gem, but every girl needs her mother's love. She notices me struggling, and she picks up her plate and comes to sit next to me.

"Hey there, love." Her energy is calming, and I'm grateful for her distraction. "What's going on? You're avoiding." For a twenty-year-old, she's very observant.

"I can't eat it, Lily."

"I know it's hard, but this is what's gonna get you home to your handsome man."

My heart breaks all over again, and I glance at the food.

"He deserves better." I suck in my breath and hold it.

"And that's why you're here, to get better."

"I hate this. I fucking hate this."

"Me too, Mama Rube. Me too."

"Back to your table, Lily," Emily interrupts us, and she compliantly slips back to her seat at table two.

Ann walks through the kitchen and bounces from patient to patient, checking in with feelings and emotions connected with the sudden shift in plans. As she comes to me, the emotion builds in my throat like water waiting for the kink to release in the hose so it can spray its pressured stream into oblivion without apology. When she's within range, I release the hose and let a stream of consciousness out that could only be compared to Old Faithful.

"Well hello, Ann. Did you come to do damage control? 'Cuz this stunt has set the tone for Manna today, and news flash, it ain't good." I hear myself and want to stop the geyser, but it's out of control.

"I can see you're upset, Ruby. Why don't you come to the porch and talk to me." Ann suggests, but my word vomit is already on its way up.

"Why, so you can keep the others calm and happy? Y'all chose this response of plating our food like we're incapable. My plate's ruined. The waffle is soggy, saturated with this shit you call grits. And I'm pretty sure I may get food poisoning from this undercooked meat. It's still fucking oinking. I'm not eating it."

Girls around me were dropping their forks, and the room got quiet. Ann asked again, "Ruby, please join me outside."

"If it gets me away from this pile of shit you call food." I stand up, and the chair's legs screech across the wood floor. I follow her loudly to the porch, and the French doors slam behind me.

"Listen, Ann, I don't know what kind of operation y'all are running here at Manna, but what you guys did to those girls in there was wrong, flat wrong. Nobody's in a good place with food in that room, and you just threw us a curveball to the face with no warning."

"There were warnings, Ruby. We've talked about the consequences of being tardy for meals."

"Like any of us can control Dillon's beauty routine!" My teeth are chattering, and tears are burning my eyes, but I refuse to let them fall.

"It's not just about Dillon, Ruby. It's about preparing for life outside of Manna. And to do that, we have to put you in real-world situations and help you through it as the emotions and fears surface."

"Is that what you're telling yourself, that you're helping them? Helping them? In what universe will I not be able to plate my own goddamn food, huh? Tell me that!" My fists are clenched along with my jaw. Every bone in my body is buzzing, and I see the gas station sign a half mile down the road and think about ghosting Ann right there. That would teach her to mess with patients.

"Can I ask you something, Ruby?"

"What?"

"Do you want to enjoy margaritas, chips, and queso with your friends?"

"I don't have friends, just people who tolerate me because it's the right thing to do."

"What about church functions and festivals? You told me that you missed being able to enjoy them in our last session."

"You can't bring up that shit. That's a HIPAA violation."

"To talk to my patient about things they said in a session that I'm trying to help make happen? Repeat my wrongdoing here."

"Why couldn't I plate my own damn waffle? Why'd you give me the most fatty bacon?"

"Ruby, what are you afraid of?"

"You're trying to make me fat!" The tears come, and I don't stop them.

"Are you scared?"

"Of being fat? Yes! Why do you think I've starved myself since I was fifteen? Read my chart before you ask me dumb shit like that, doc. Oh, excuse me, *dietitian*."

"What's bad about having fat on your body?"

"You're skinny, so your bullshit psychology isn't gonna work on me."

"Ruby, answer the question."

"I don't know!"

"You don't know what?"

"I don't know why I'm scared! I just want to be fucking normal. Not fat, not skinny, just fucking normal, you know? I don't want to feel this anymore. I don't want to be in this panic mode anytime one tiny thing doesn't go my way! I once had a panic attack holding doughnuts for Michael's grandmother's funeral reception. You hear that? A panic attack because I was holding doughnuts. The fuck if I was going to eat them, but I'm that messed up that I couldn't regain my composure to go back to the service. Michael had to face the death of his grandma without his wife because she was losing it over holding fucking doughnuts. She is me, Ann. She is me." I back up to the wall and slowly slide down it and hug my knees as I sink further into the ground.

Ann takes a seat beside me. "She is worthy of living in the light of the life she's created without fear of food, don't you think?"

"Yeah, she does."

"You do."

"I do."

"See, we agree."

"It's a miracle." I lift my head and look out over the yard. My furry friend is waiting for my failure.

"I think I want to drink margaritas."

"Yeah?" Ann asks. "Salt or no salt?"

"On the rocks, with salt."

"Sounds amazing."

"Yeah."

"Can we start with waffles?"

"I guess," I add. "I'm sorry I yelled at you."

"You're forgiven, Ruby. I really want to see you get that margarita."

"Me too," I say, and I walk back to the table and sit down and take a bite of cold, soggy waffle.

*****

To continue the extended torture, we hear Emily call out that the afternoon snack will now be changed to a challenge snack, and my heart sinks for the umpteenth time today. Challenge snack is something we do twice a week. It's normal snack time, but there's a twist each time that we don't know the catch until we walk into the dining room. For the second time today, we've been bamboozled. What's next? Give the gremlins water after midnight and see who's left standing? I hate that creepy movie. Check on the '80s kids in your life. They're still scared of leprechauns, labyrinths, and anything giant, hairy, and just enough human tendencies to straddle fantasy and reality. I don't care who you are. The late '80s and early '90s films were traumatizing!

I can still see Benji running from the wolf.

"What torture are we enduring now?" a woman asked what all of us were thinking.

"New snack challenge!" Emily yells, and we reluctantly take our seats. One girl is already crying, and another is refusing to comply, and Dr. Leslie is escorting her to the porch for a pep talk.

Been there.

At breakfast, in fact.

"Today, you must pick something from the kitchen you've never had here at Manna House before."

Dillon whispers to me, "How's she gonna know what we've eaten?" but her whisper is a normal volume to most, so Emily hears her and follows up.

"We keep track of all your snacks and meals, so don't try to pull any fast ones on us." She glares at Dillon.

"Dangit!" Dillon doesn't even attempt to whisper with that one, and I nudge her foot under the table. She opens her hazel eyes wide, as if she's shocked that I would correct her, but she calls me Mama Rube for a reason. "What? She couldn't have possibly heard me!" And she sucked her teeth in annoyance.

I should be home parenting my own kids.

Emily interrupts my thoughts. "Table one, come on up and choose a new exciting snack! Her words are dripped in sarcasm as always, and I get up and head to the fridge to attempt to create the lightest, safest new choice. I scan the contents of the icebox as I feel other anxious eyes taking stock at the same time. Emily walks up beside me, and she shoots her shot at moving me along. "Anything you haven't had yet that looks yummy?"

I feel like a toddler, and I want to smack the shit out of her forced smile. I know this is what she's hired to do, and I know she's only trying to help, but it doesn't make the urge to throw her off a cliff diminish one bit. I scan the fridge for the seventh time, and I feel Dillon's hand on my shoulder.

"Wanna have some cottage cheese and fruit with me, Mama Rube? We can suffer in solidarity!"

Solidarity is a big buzzword around here, and I never knew its value until I came to Manna House. One thing about eating disorders, they thrive in the dark, and they feed off being alone. I never really saw how much my own actions and behaviors connected with food seeped into everyone in my vicinity because I'd never had a mirror held to me as I experienced the episodes. Now that I'm surrounded by others who think and behave like me, I sure as hell get it. Being saturated with other's emotions and actions around food anxiety and obsession is exhausting and all-consuming. I think about Michael and the kids and cringe.

I'm here.

That counts for something.

Having someone to go through a challenging meal with you and actually *get it* is priceless. I'll never undervalue the significance of being afraid, having someone understand that fear, and hold your hand through it the entire way. I've always been shamed for my thoughts and feelings on food, but I know anyone that has made comments spoke them from a place of deep love and blissful ignorance.

Except this one arrogant guy I worked with.

He's an asshole.

Many people have experienced disordered eating habits, but having an eating disorder is not the same thing. One is sticking a toe in the icy water and deciding, nah, this ain't for me. The other is climbing a bridge, opening your heart to the sky, and swan diving headfirst into the shallow creek that will saturate your lifeless body as you slowly float down the river, escaping the wolves that pace the banks thinking, *Ha, I've won,* but really, the grave is the only one left fulfilled.

"Yeah, sure." I'm brought back to the challenge: cottage cheese and fruit.

"What fruit do you want? I'm adding pineapple." Dillon takes a quarter cup of tangy morsels, and my mouth fills with saliva, preparing for the imminent snack. It's crazy the little things that have already come back to me after a week of proper nourishment after years of abuse. Number one, I got my period on the third day I was here. Emily reassured me it was a good thing, but part of me felt like an ED failure. I hadn't had a period since I was seventeen years old. The doctors were shocked that I ever got pregnant once, much less twice as bad as my disorder was.

The second normal body function that's back is hunger. People've always questioned how I was never hungry even though I never ate. I didn't know how to explain it, but I just never felt hunger cues, so it was easy to avoid eating. Ann said that's a normal defense mechanism the body creates in starvation. That way, you slowly shut down, blissfully unaware of the agony that's going on inside of you. My body learned to function on a calorie deficit for years, and it was now finally learning to trust that it would be getting fed regularly. I feel the rumble start, and it makes me sad.

Is my ED gone now?

I didn't even get to say goodbye.

"I'll try the dried cranberries." I grab the container and the measuring cup. I dig it into the hardened wrinkled berries and slop them on top of the cup of cottage cheese. It sounds like the splat of Hudson's hand in a thick mudhole, and it makes my throat constrict in retaliation.

Oh, hey, there you are, ED.

The chunks of lumpy cheese throughout the soupy white liquid looks like a cyst I watched being popped on a show, and I cover my mouth in a desperate attempt to keep lunch from coming up. Puking is definitely against the rules, and I don't want to start a riot. But my stomach still thinks food is the enemy, so I feel like there's a brick in it at all times eating this much this frequently. I regain control, walk to the table with my challenge, and sit next to Dillon reluctantly. She reaches under the table and grabs my leg and gives it a squeeze. Her smile is warm, and she digs into the bowl in front of her with ease.

My turn.

That's how solidarity works.

I dip my spoon in the concoction, fold in the cranberries, and attempt to hide them completely. I'm regretting my snack decision before I even try it, and I'm tempted to ask Emily to pick something else, but I know she'll only say it's against the rules, so I take a bite.

Holy fucking shit.

I allow the chunks of cheese to slide across my tongue like molten lava pushing rock and dirt against their consent, and the path of destruction is creamy and sour. I bite down to chew the sugar-saturated berries, and the consistency of their flesh glues my teeth together, squishing out the chunks of curdled cheese through the gaps in my teeth to settle in the pockets of my cheeks like a chipmunk.

I'm gonna puke.

I attempt to swallow my new number one enemy, but my esophagus refuses to let it pass. I heave, retch, and spit out the shit excuse for food onto my place mat I made during free time the first night here. Although it was not my first choice for a nighttime ritual, anything was better than allowing the black hole in my chest to consume me in front of fifteen other struggling strangers.

I can't eat this.

"Mama Rube, you all right?" Dillon and all the others are staring at me in horror. One person losing it in a treatment center is as deadly as the plague, and I see Emily coming to intervene before more damage is done.

"Ruby, you all right? Wanna talk about it?" She's trying to be patient, but I sense her disgust.

"I can't eat this."

"You can't, or you won't?" she challenges me, and it pisses me off.

"Just because I'm disordered doesn't mean I don't have taste buds. This is disgusting." I put down my fork in defiance.

"You chose it, Ruby. You have to eat it."

"The fuck I do," I say, and it shocks me, but it feels right to fight.

"Ruby, I urge you to eat the snack. There are going to be times in life that the choices are not ideal, but you need to nourish your body regardless."

"I've made it this far starving, so your fake-ass scenarios mean nothing to me." I practically spit at her, but she smiles and continues to push.

"It's not fake, Ruby. Sometimes, you'll have to compromise and eat to honor your body's need for fuel."

"Again, I've made it this far, thank you, so kindly excuse me while I throw this shit excuse for food away." I stood up and grabbed my bowl, and at the same time, Emily used my napkin to wipe the spit-out slop off my place mat to reveal two sweet faces staring up at me. I close my eyes, tears well up, and I'm beat before she even speaks.

"Do it for your kids if you can't do it for yourself."

My kids...

"That's so dirty." I wipe the overflow from my cheeks but don't give her the satisfaction of the sob that's creeping up my throat.

"Just trying to help." And she walks away to let me make my own decision.

I stare at my sweet children's faces. The picture is of them sitting in the concrete mixing bin that I turned into a sled to pull them around the yard on, and it's their favorite thing to do right now. Their faces are covered in sunflower seeds, and their little grins are chunkier than the cottage cheese in front of me. Their smiles can light up the darkest of hearts.

I hope Michael knows the route around the yard.

I sit back down, and I can feel all eyes are on me. The whole dining room is waiting to see my next move, and it hits me. All the women here are just little kids too, kids who are looking for direction and leadership to guide them to safety, and if I lose it, the aftermath of the meltdown will ripple through the masses and poison the water of the whole group. I have to eat this fucking snack.

I can't be the reason others fail.

I'm sick of being the problem.

I pick up my spoon and let it hover over the disgusting mush. I dip the tip of it in the cheese and move my tongue across the bridge of my mouth to generate saliva, but my mouth's bone-dry.

Do it for Nali and Hud.

I close my eyes and dig in. The texture is enough to make me gag, but the sour creamy lava's got to go down this time. I swallow the first spoonful, and I look up to stop the tears. I see the wolf in his usual spot out the window, and I hope it's taking a good hard look. With each mouthful, I'm eating *his* meal. I'm feeding the alpha of the pack now, and that alpha is *me*.

As I see the bottom of the bowl, I stop and look around. Their eyes were on me, all of them. The binge eater who's trying to see her worth while singing "Manic Monday" on repeat to dredge up any serotonin she has left. The anorexic who's fighting like hell to win over her ED that screams in her sleep; those screams are palpable. The recovering addict who traded needles for laxatives; she's in the fight of her life, but I'm not worried; that bitch can throw hands. The skeleton of a girl whose robotic posture that's painful to witness, who allowed herself to dance to "22" like she saw the glimmer of hope that living a life without fear is possible.

I know I'm the archetype usually portrayed in the anorexic role, but despite that irony, eating disorders don't discriminate. People of any age, race, religion, sex, gender, education—the list goes on—can fall prey to this monster. What's special about this group? Nothing. There's nothing special about these women. They are the same as all of us. These are women fighting battles that generations before them created, but they're left to deal with the aftermath. A woman's relationship with her body is an ancient feud that's been passed down like a dominant gene from mother to daughter and daughter to granddaughter. It's a never-ending cycle that won't stop until someone says enough is enough.

I've had enough.

I'm sad in a way I never imagined, and their pained faces flip a switch in my brain. It clicked. I don't want this. I don't fucking want this. I don't want anyone to experience this shame, pain, and agony that I have connected with food, and I know what I need to do.

I picture Bruce in Roald Dahl's *Matilda* with Trunchbull's cake. I hear the brave Matilda begin the chant,

"Brucey, Brucey, Brucey," and he takes the challenge on with a renewed vigor. He fights past the pain and agony, and he consumes the chocolate monster, coming out the victor in the students' fight against the injustices of Trunchbull's regime. And then the bitch breaks the glass platter over his head, and he crumbles like the glass around him to the floor. And then, despite her attempt to break him, he gets up. Cheers of the students roar just for him because Bruce has achieved his hero status standing up to the bully who calls herself their principal.

Solidarity, Bruce.

I scrape the last bit of sour milk out of the bottom of the bowl and pick out the last cranberry out with my fingers and pop it in my chalky mouth. As I chew, I look at the smiling faces on my place mat, and I'm suddenly thankful for stupid nighttime crafts. I place my napkin on the table, tip my bowl to Emily so she can see my victory, and walk it to the sink. I turn on the water to rinse the contents and look out the sink window that looks over a garden and the pecan trees in the distance. I see a familiar figure sauntering toward the woods with its tail between his legs.

Ruby, Ruby, Ruby.

*****

That night, it was quiet enough to hear a heartbeat in our bedroom. Dillon was reading her Bible, and I was reading "The River," a short story by my favorite author Flannery O'connor. The rawness of her broken and searching characters resonates with my soul, and I read them for comfort like someone who watches *The Office* on repeat for background noise. It's a story about a boy named Harry, who doesn't know Jesus, but he knows neglect. When a random babysitter takes him to a baptism, the preacher's promise of a better life in the kingdom of heaven begins only with a dunk in the river, and Harry's all in. The outcome's not what he envisioned because he ends up going back to his negligent parents' apartment, where he's a nobody, and decides to take matters in his own hands. The ending is a brutal shock to the system that will haunt your soul, and it makes you question humanity on a deep level, but Harry's finally free and makes it to the kingdom of heaven despite a failed first attempt.

Right now, I feel like Harry. I'm trusting complete strangers with my recovery, and if they're wrong, I'll pay with my life. If they're right, I imagine it will feel like heaven and earth collided just to celebrate my decision to thrive, not survive.

I hope I don't drown.

"Mama Rube, you okay?" Dillon is already makeup-free and tucked in while I've been stuck in the same position reading and not ready for bed since evening free time.

"Not really." I'm honest. If treatment's taught me anything, it's that the truth will always come out. It's better for all involved to just start with it.

"What do you need?" I know she's sincere. I think about it.

"A hug," I confess. I realized after the words left my mouth that I hadn't been touched by another human in seven days. I went from being touched and needed constantly to isolated and alone in the time it takes the sun to dip below the horizon and hide from the cruel world.

Without even asking, Dillon crawled into bed with me. She nuzzled up behind me, and my body fit into her half-moon shape with ease. She wrapped her arms around me. She smelled good, like cocoa butter and toothpaste, and she nestled her chin in the crease between my neck and my shoulder.

"I'm the big spoon, Mama Rube. Just take it."

Her embrace reminds me of Michael's strong arms holding me together. Her embrace reminds me of rocking Hudson for hours as an infant because his acid reflux burned, and I prayed for God to give his pain to me. Her embrace reminds me of Nali's need for connection and physical touch that I can't give her due to my own bodily hang-ups. How am I going to raise a strong and confident woman when I fall short in the self-love department daily?

"Dillon, do you love your mom?"

"My mom is the shit."

"Do you blame her for your disorder?"

"Hell no. I'm the fucking problem."

"Do you think my kids are gonna hate me for leaving them to come here?"

She squeezes tighter, and I'm glad she doesn't let go. "Mama Rube, one day they're gonna thank you for fighting. I guarantee."

"How do you know?"

"Because that's how it works. We love our parents so deeply, and when we realize that all they went through to get you to this point, you forgive the bullshit and are just thankful you have someone that tried their best to be the best version of themselves for your benefit. There's no greater love than that."

I let her words seep in like the grits in the waffle. Maybe she's right. Maybe they'll see all I sacrifice one day and thank me for not giving up.

"Is Michael coming for visitation Sunday?"

I swallow hard. "Yes."

"Are the kids coming?"

My teeth chatter, and I look to the ceiling to regain control. "No, we decided that it'll scare them to see me here more than help them."

"Probably right."

"Dillon, can you hold me a little longer?" I suck in a sob.

"Yeah, Mama. I'm right here."

"Thanks." I hear the toenails of the beast clicking on the linoleum, and I allow Dillon's embrace to be my shield. We thrive in numbers, or we fail alone.

I don't want to be alone anymore.

The wolves don't count.

CHAPTER 14

Sunday, March 6, 2016

The sweat is pooling at the arches of my feet, and my back is soggy in the sheets, and I look at the clock for the seventh time: 4:25 a.m. No surprise there.

Speaking of surprises, it seems as if I've reached the night sweats part of the Recovery Games. I'm sopping wet, and there's still so long until 7:00 a.m. I shift in the bleached linens, and the screech of fabric makes Dillon turn over with a few snorts.

Okay, I should tell the whole truth of my insomnia this morning. There's two loose ends that need to be tied up, wires that need to be mended in the fence to protect the sheep and keep the wolves at bay: my parents and Marco.

It's visiting day, and my dad and Michael are coming. Dad's here to meet with Dr. Leslie and me to help me transition back into the family with care and ease. Although I'm not ready to reenter the world of the living quite yet, I want to give my family the time they deserve to prepare to meet the new Ruby.

No.

That's not right.

The *real* Ruby Blue.

I'm still trying to find her, but I know this. I'm going to protect my peace every step of the way until I get there. How long will that take? Until. It's that simple. Until. We are all works of progress in this universe that is an ombré rainbow of all the water that connects us all to both God and Mother Nature. What a blessing to those who chose to chase that pot of gold *until*. I think about the life I want to live, and that's it. That's the way. Chase your pot of gold, and the road will always have purpose, hope, and love. That's all I want—purpose, hope, and love.

Speaking of love, I get to hold Michael today. I get to hold him and tell him *I'm sorry*. All these years, he's held on to me, and he's taken the brunt of the blows all because he vowed to love me, from day one, for the rest of my life. And even after all I've put him through, he's never broken that vow.

I remember sitting on the porch of my last apartment in Starkville, Mississippi. It was off Maxwell Street across from Bin 612, and it was the old Kappa Alpha house from the '80s that someone turned into three apartments. Three guys and a bulldog named MacGyver lived in the basement of the house, one guy lived on the main level, and I lived in the attic. To say it was small would be kind. It wasn't even big enough to do a forward roll in, much less a cartwheel. I had a bed, a sink, a shower, a stove, and a love seat, and those small items took up one hundred percent of the floor space. The ceiling was vaulted, and not like "*ooh,* ah" vaulted but "nightmare A-frame that almost gave me three concussions" vaulted. I'm about to go all Sonnet 130 on you here, though, because even though it was a nightmare, it was the first place I ever lived on my own and where I fell in love with Michael.

I don't remember the time or date, and that bothers me, but I do remember the sky that night. It was a deep black, the kind that almost looks purple with dimmed streetlights glowing. The stars were given the spotlight because God's thumbnail was glowing just enough to reassure us of his presence. I was on the porch with my phone pressed to my ear. Michael and I had been arguing about what was the better way to eat baked goods: hot or cold? I said hot because I remember Charleigh, Naomi, and I being too impatient to wait until everything was cooled and chowed down. His mom made him and his brother wait, so he's grown up the opposite.

Funny how you have to adapt and accept even the littlest things when you commit to loving a person authentically.

As we were bantering, my heart had hope. It had direction. It had peace. I wanted it to have those things forever and have those things with the guy on the other side of the line. It was that night I told Michael I loved him, and he said it back.

And here I am now, only eleven days into treatment and already feeling a power I never thought I'd achieve due to chronic self-sabotage. I mean, it was me *all this time.* I had a crippling fear of being abandoned, and it left me to navigate this life alone because to me, alone was better than being left against my will. But it's different now. I'm not a scared seven-year-old anymore. I've created the life I wanted as a child, and I have to start believing that I'm worthy of living it. I can parent Nali and Hudson the way I feel is best. I can own my feelings, limits, and boundaries without feeling like I'm letting someone down. I can have a marriage that doesn't fail because there are two parties involved in it who're willing to do the necessary work. Now it's my turn to let go of this shit that I've used to escape and trust no matter what, God's always given me angels to navigate difficult times in life, and through all those tests, trials, and tribulations, I've been carried. For those angels, I'm forever grateful.

*****

It's 11:00 a.m., and I have a session with Dr. Leslie. She said it's time to talk about Marco.

Ugh.

As I sat on her couch, waiting for her to come in, I felt the sweat pooling in my Chacos. I put Marco in the past a long time ago, but he's never left my subconscious.

"Good morning, Mrs. Ruby Blue! Are you excited to see your family today? Who's all coming?" She pauses and puts her hand over her mouth. "Excuse me for assuming they are." She backtracks, and I cringe a bit thinking about her seemingly small slipup.

I'm so thankful I can be on the you-assumed-correctly part of this conversation because there are many girls here at Manna House who will not get visitors today…or ever. One woman's been here seven months, and her family's barely able to pay for the treatment, much less the travel, so she sits alone Sunday after Sunday, watching others embrace their loved ones while she knits and pets Hermosita the Manna House cat. Don't even get me started on the cost of treatment. I already know I'll be working three jobs to pay this shit off.

Anyone hiring?

Others will get visitors that they wish would've just stayed home. Eating disorder behaviors are often learned, and it's never difficult to spot the tree after you discover the apple. Trees tend to grow in clusters and add more and more apples to the lot over time. The great qualities and aspects that we love about the apples we watch nature cultivate are

205

praised and prized, but one bad mutation can spoil the harvest. Many people who are trying to recover are going back into the toxic environment that helped get them here, so recovery often depends on the support system that is selfless enough to take a hard look at their own contribution with the purpose of healing, not shaming.

I'm blessed.

My family's selfless.

Thank-you will never be enough.

"Yep, my dad's coming for lunch, and then Michael's coming this afternoon."

"Great, I'm so glad! But first, we have to talk about Marco."

"Do we *have* to talk about Marco?"

"Yes, ma'am. Don't you want him to stop stealing the lead role in your dreams?"

"Sometimes they're good, you know what I'm sayin'?"

"Michael's job, not your messed-up memory of Marco's."

"Touché."

"Why do you think you dream about him?"

"Because he was a significant person in my life that I put too much trust into too young, and he came at a time when I was searching for any proof that people can stay together and stay in love. I was sixteen, I was ignorant, and I was reckless. I've got to let go of the rules and regulations that it took to keep a man that was never mine in the first place and move on."

"Wow. Are we doing what we talked about last week?"

"Did you get the case?"

"I sure did."

"Did you print the picture?"

"I did that as well."

"Then let's do this."

The sun is high, and it's the perfect day to soak it up like a cat, but I can't. I've got work to do. I brought out my phone and headphones to get in the zone, and I carried the case of Sprite to the tree line out back and hung the portrait on the stone wall that edges the east side of the property. The wolf knows better than to show up today, so I'm relaxed and confident as I walk about fifteen steps back and turn toward the wall.

Why do I have Sprites and an eight-by-ten picture of my first love?

Because I have unfinished business.

The last time I saw Marco was when I was nineteen at an old high school friend's party after my first semester at State. I was talking with a few people, and Marco waltzed up, his charming half smile in full force. We got together and broke up so many times, who knows what episode of the Ruby and Marco Show we were on, but that confrontation would be the series finale.

"Hey there, Ruby. Long time no see. Thought you'd be knee-deep in catfish ponds in the Delta? Glad us city friends get graced with your presence, Ms. Mississippi Queen." His tone is as condescending as ever, and I see him stumble a bit into his James Dean lean. It used to do it for me, but now it just seemed sad.

"Hey, Marco, and I'm just here for Christmas. Heading back to Starkvegas on the twenty-sixth." I shift my weight on the other hip, and I see him eye me up and down.

"Looks like you've really gone downhill since we called it quits." He reached for my can of Sprite and examined the nutrition label.

"Excuse me?" I don't know why I'm acting surprised. Ever since he's achieved a twelve pack and pecs bigger than my tits, he's been a complete ass to me.

He tossed the can in the trash and looked dead into my eyes one last time before I'd never let him again. "You'll thank me later."

He walked away, and I did nothing. I said nothing to defend myself, and I let his words seep into my soul like the toxic slop he fed me for so long. Instead of throwing his shit right back at him, I took it…over and over again.

Well, Marco, it's later, and I've never said thank you, so here's my tribute to you.

"Are you all set?" Dr. Leslie asks as she hands me a pair of safety glasses as if an aluminum can bouncing back and hitting me in the face would be solved with ten cents' worth of plastic. I put them on so I can't sue Manna, and we can get along with the experiment.

"Very ready." I hold the cold can in my palm, feeling its weight with a shake.

"Okay, remember, physical release can trigger mental release if we allow it, and we want to use helpful, not harmful purging, so imagine Marco's poison that he spewed at you for years explode on that wall with that can and leave it in the sun to evaporate. His opinions of you, your body, and what you eat are no longer Ruby's law."

Those last words hit me hard, and my throat constricts. Until I got to Manna, I didn't realize how much Marco's constant conditions and expectations of appearance and body were poisoning my brain. His fad diets, constant workouts, and unrealistic expectations of fitness became my law too, and I allowed it. I also allowed his law to stick with me all the way to age thirty-one. I haven't seen or talked to Marco in twelve years, but I hear his voice in my head daily, sometimes hourly, and he comes to me in my sleep and breaks me over and over again for fun.

Marco's reign ends today.

I position my feet so that my left shoulder is pointed at the tree. I take the can and stretch it slowly behind my back, turn, and throw a rainbow lob that hits the ground before the target, and Marcos's half smile makes me boil.

"Get mad, Ruby. Let it out. Now's the time." Dr. Leslie prompts, and her point is clear as crystal. I shuffle through my playlist until I hear the familiar sound of our song's beginning.

It's the Tim and Faith song "It's Your Love" that once represented such a fear-based bond, and now that I listen to the words, it actually fits perfectly. Go look up the lyrics. Now only if Ozzy Osbourne were singing it with a gothic, eerie melody that I could work with.

I throw another can, now with more vigor and purpose. The can flips end over end and makes contact right above Marco's head. The spray of the Sprite looks like the fireworks over Lake Oconee on the Fourth of July. The remaining liquid crawls down the photo, and it reminds me of racing the raindrops on the car window when I was a kid.

That felt really good.

I wing another one, and it hits his forehead this time and leaves a dent in the photo paper as proof.

Once I got the hang of the first two, the next nine followed suit. Exploding carbonated soda and destroyed cans went flying one after another after another. I threw each one harder the first, and the eleventh can flung from my hand, and I swear it broke the rock behind what was left of Marco's face. The soaking wet, tattered picture succumbed to the battle and fell to the wet earth below.

I have one can left, and I rear back to throw it, but the picture's gone. The moment's passed. I look for the wolf to give him his, but it's not here.

I do the next thing that pops into my head. I crack open the Sprite, put the cold aluminum to my bottom lip, part my mouth, and let the bubbles hit the back of my throat and tickle my nose in a familiar sensation. I cover my mouth and nose and bend over, trying not to spit it out. I actually want to swallow this. I want to consume every last drop.

As I hold the empty can above my open mouth, I stick out my tongue as if to catch the tiniest of snowflakes. My taste buds are buzzing in a good way, and I realize I'm smiling. Dr. Leslie begins a slow clap, and I drop the can and smash it with my shoe. It seemed way too *Road House*, but I've always loved the soft side of Swayze.

"How'd that feel?"

"Incredible."

"I'll never look at Sprite the same again."

"Me neither."

Goodbye, Marco.

Don't come back.

*****

It's 2:00 p.m., and visitation starts now. Any minute, the crinkle and pop of the gravel lot will send necks craning to see whose loved one has arrived. I don't care about anything right now. I just need to see my dad.

I've hid the severity of my disorder from my family as much as possible over the years, but my last six-month decline exposed my battle. I lost my ability to function as a normal human because I was in my head constantly arguing with my demons and running from the wolves. I was down to a weight that's not even fit for a preteen, and the monster that once gave me instructions from the shadows was using me as a voice to spew his hate and fear. I'm embarrassed by my actions, and I'm terrified that the damage Hurricane Ruby made in her wake may be too extensive to repair this time.

I see the same silver sedan that's been the relieving sign that backup's here, and every fiber of my body suddenly wants to crumble. He pulls into the closest spot, and I see the car jolt in park. The front door opens, and my tried and true emerges. He's the definition of unconditional love, and I've never felt otherwise. My legs feel weak, but I make my way to the front walk to see my dad.

I see him walking fast, his legs moving twice the rate as his arms swing, and then he breaks into a jog. I just crumble. I collapsed right there on the stone walk, but my dad was there to catch me. He cradled my body like he did when I fell off my bike, and a wail left the depths of my gut, and his arms grip me even tighter. I hear his sobs and feel the heaves of his chest. The guilt of what I'm putting him through is enough to make me want to die.

"Oh, Ruby Leigh. Oh my Ruby Leigh. My girl, my girl." He was repeating that over and over again through muffled sobs, and the little rock back and forth felt like home. I'm sure we were a sight: a sixty-one-year-old man holding his thirty-one-year-old daughter on the front walk of a mental hospital, but for the first time, I couldn't care less. There's no age cutoff of the love between a parent and a child, and yes, it does shift, but that relationship is always a beautiful journey. My dad's always shown up, and today may be his most important appearance to date.

"Hey dad." It's all I can manage at the moment, but it's enough.

"How's my girl?"

"Better."

"I'm so glad." He sits me up, and his blue eyes are as clear as the spring sky. It reminds me of the classic phrase "April showers bring May flowers," and I think that's true for most things in life. The storms we face make us appreciate the sunshine and blue sky a bit more, and sometimes there's even a rainbow. We walk over to the bench in front of the garden, and I see another girl run down the sidewalk to her parents, and I wipe the wet off my face with my hoodie sleeve.

"Thank you for coming."

"I wouldn't miss it for the world. You kidding me?"

"Do you think the others are mad I didn't want them to come?" My lips tremble, scared of the answer.

"Oh, Ruby, we all are just so proud of you for getting the help you truly need. No one is anything but proud. Pat, your mom, Charleigh." I can't. He continues, "Naomi, Robert." I'm gonna lose it. "Michael, Hudson, Nali—we're all here for you. We're nervous too. This is scary for all of us, but we're gonna get you through it together, okay? You're gonna be okay, Ruby Leigh, you're gonna be okay." He silently wipes his cheeks as the tears continue to flow.

"I don't deserve your support. I should've never let it get this bad, Dad! I hate myself for putting everyone through this. What kind of person can do that to their kids, Dad? What kind of mother can knowingly harm herself and them, Dad? I don't deserve them. They deserve better than me."

His arms squeezed me tightly, and I didn't fight it. I went from having two cats, two kids, and a husband on me 24-7 to only one "big spoon, little spoon" encounter with Dillon since I've been here. This is the best hug I've ever received, and I know I'll feel it for a lifetime.

"Ruby, as a dad, it's hard to describe what I'm feeling at the moment, but let me try." He has one arm around me and one wiping his tears, and we're both staring ahead for survival. "I was so nervous pulling in here because I didn't know what to expect, but I knew that if you needed me to, I would knock the front door down to get to you." He sniffs. "And it's never felt better to hold you. As your parents, it's impossible for your mom and I to watch our daughter suffer and feel as though it's our fault."

"Dad."

"Let me finish. We know the divorce was hard on you as a kid, and we carry a lot of guilt connected with that. We were so young, so green, and I know we made mistakes, but we always tried to do our best for you girls."

"I know, Dad."

"I just kick myself for not doing something sooner. I knew you were in trouble. I knew I needed to step in."

"It's not your job to fix me, Dad. It's mine. I'm the only one in control of me and my actions, so please don't say that. It's not your fault."

"Easier said than done, Ruby. You just wait until—"

"That's why I'm here, Dad, for them."

"And *that's* why we're proud."

"I love you, Dad. Thanks for always showing up."

He sucked in a sob and squeezed me tightly. "Now go introduce me to that cat friend of yours."

My dad loves cats too.

*****

It's closing in on five o'clock, and Hermosita gives me a warning bite because I'm petting her too much. Being an eating disorder therapy pet has its perks because we talk about setting clear boundaries often. Hermacita has caught on. Michael should be here any second, and my heart is in my stomach. The last time I saw him, my ED face was screaming at him, "*Don't make me do this. Don't make me fucking do this!*" and I crumbled as he opened the car door to assist me out like the many times I passed out before.

If I'm honest, I'm scared, scared that the past eleven days have shown him how amazing life is without my eating disorder fucking things up for him and the kids. I picture the three of them laughing and joking at dinner rather than me crying and causing a scene. I picture hair being braided with bows and milk mustaches being wiped, not dipping out for tennis shoes and pavement. I picture joy and peace without my turmoil and chaos, and I'm scared Michael will see it too.

The crackle and pop of the gravel makes Hermosita jump. I look up to see the familiar beat-up, Vegas Gold Pontiac Montana we bought from his grandparents. They used to drive their Amish neighbors to doctors' appointments in Hershey, Pennsylvania. The treatment bill has broken us. Literally in every sense, but financially, we're drowning. We took out a medical loan, sold the car, sold all the baby furniture and clothes, and took Hudson's savings to pay for it. I'll never forget being in the kitchen and taking down his mason jar of cash that he'd saved over his four short years of life. All the holiday cards from his unkie, grandma, and grandpa added up, and I felt like the lowest human on the face of the earth having to take it. What happened next was the lowest moment of my life.

"Mama?" I hear his voice as I'm counting out the bills I just stole from his money jar.

No...

Michael steps in. "Hey, Hud, what are you doing up, my guy?"

"I had to go to the bathroom." His lips were pouty like his Aunt Charleigh's when she's tired, and he rubs his eyes open before I can put up the evidence. "What are you doing counting my money?"

"Mama's counting it to see how close you are to—"

"Stop, Michael." I couldn't do it anymore. I couldn't keep lying to Hudson. He knows everything that comes out of my mouth is bullshit these days, and I remember feeling that way as a kid. I knew when my parents lied to me. Their lies made me distrust and learn to lie to tell people what they want to hear instead of owning the truth and living in the light of the reality that we're all human and make mistakes. Right now, I'm suffering, and Hudson sees that no matter how good of an actor I believe I may be.

I've yet to get a callback.

"Hud, I want to tell you what's going on." I look up and summon all the mama strength I can, and I kneel down and motion for him to come sit on my knee. He does, and he is immediately squirming because my bones are digging into his quads. I stand him up in front of me and look into his hazel eyes that mirror his dad's. I'm done lying. I'd rather mess him up and have him know the real me than ever blame any of the shit I'll inevitably pass on to him on himself.

"Mama's going to go away for a while, but I'll be back, and I'll be better than ever."

His lip quivers, and his chest fills with air to pillow the tears. "No, Mama."

"Yeah, buddy, I've got to go to get some help."

"Help with what?"

"Help with becoming a better mama for you and your sister."

"But you're already a good mama. You're the best mama."

"I'm so glad to hear you say that, Hud, but I need to go so I can learn to love myself as much as you, Nali, and Daddy love me. I want to love myself like that.

"Daddy can help. You can stay here, and Daddy can fix you. He fixed my bed this morning when it was broken, and now it doesn't squeak anymore. He's magic!"

I looked at Michael, and he had his hand covering his nose and mouth. "Yes, Hudson, Daddy is magic. We all are!

Your Nana taught me a long time ago that everyone has the power inside them to heal. All we have to do is want to live our best life and go for it. She always told me to *find the gift,* and I have to go find mine. Daddy's done so much to help me already, and now I have to go learn from professionals that are gonna teach me to love myself like you love me because that's the best love I know."

He cocks his head like a sled dog waiting for a command, but his question catches me off guard. "Who'll clean the litter box? Do I have to do it now?"

"No, buddy, Daddy will take care of that."

"Okay. How long will you be gone?"

"I don't know, but I'm going to do everything in my power to learn all the things so I can get back to you as soon as I can. You hear me? I'm gonna get better. I promise."

I promise.

"What were you doing with my money?"

Oof. "Well, I need to borrow it."

"For what?"

I swallow hard. "To help pay for the classes I'm taking. They're expensive, and I will pay you back as soon as I can, bud."

"So it's for your mama school?"

"Yeah."

"Okay, then, as long as you pay me back."

"You've got a deal. Thanks for understanding, Hud."

"No problem."

As he walked up the stairs that night, I swear I saw a wolf-like shadow follow him around the corner.

The gold monster's loud creak as Michael slams the front door shut startles both Hermacita and me, and I stand up to allow the blood to flow to my feet. My leggings are actually fitting these days, so I don't have to pull them up, and it feels good not to hurt to sit on a wooden porch. I have a ways to go, but my heart's not stopping in my sleep, so that's a start.

I see flowers in his hand, and I suddenly can't breathe. As the lump in my throat threatens to choke me, I start to sprint. I can hear Emily bitching to me about it later, but right now, I don't care. My best friend's here, and I need to feel his arms around me.

He stops, I collide, and then I crumble in an ugly cry for the second time in three hours. I mean, this must be my Oscar moment because it's not often that a woman gets to have a *Homeward Bound* moment with both her dad and husband on the same day.

It's my moment.

And it's perfect.

Michael's strong hands cradle my head, and I smell the house on his clothes, and it makes me swallow hard. I missed his arms around me. I let the tears come, and I didn't stop myself from weeping. One thing I've learned at Manna is that emotions come in waves. If you ride them out instead of trying to stop them, you'll allow nature's process to unfold instead of contradicting every cell in your body. I'm allowing my body to feel, release, and move on, and I can feel its gratitude in response.

"Hey, Rubes," he whispers into my ear.

"Hey, Michael," I breathe into his chest.

"I missed you." I feel his arms squeeze tighter.

"I missed you more."

"The kids miss you too, babe. They miss you so much." I hear his voice shaking, and I feel his chin bouncing on my shoulder.

"I hope they'll know one day that I did this for them."

"Oh, babe, they'll know. Hudson told me to tell you that Panda ate a bird, and Murphie won't stop putting her butt in our faces when we read stories at bedtime."

"I can't believe I'm saying these words, but I wish I had a Murphie ass in my face right now."

"She'd be jealous of this fluff ball here, for sure. You've made a friend here, and it's a cat. Why am I not surprised?" He dropped an arm to pet Hermacita as she sniffed before giving approval. She decides he's okay, rolls on her back, and does the perfect cat flop to give him her belly as proof. "She's showin' off, Mama." His smile is so big that I can barely see his eyes.

"I'm sorry, Michael. I'm so sorry for all of this."

"Ruby, the worst and best day of my life was the day I dropped you off at Manna House."

"I can see the 'worst day' part, but 'best day'? You've lost me there."

"It was the worst because I felt like I was throwing you to the wolves."

I see my friend's shadow pacing the tree line.

"It was also the best because I finally felt like I was not the only one responsible for your well-being, you know? For so long, I fought your demons with little to no help, and I trust Dr. Sapphire and the staff here at Manna. They're people here that know what to do, and I'm so grateful to leave you in the hands of professionals so you can actually get rid of your ED."

"But it's taking me from you and the kids."

"Only so we can have you for a lifetime! Gah, Ruby, these next few months of hell will give our family a chance at heaven."

"Thank you, Michael." I suck in a sob and wipe my face on my sleeve.

"Thank you for fighting, Rubes. Now let's eat. I want to meet this Dillon I've heard so much about."

"It's tofu night."

"What's that?"

"Don't worry about it. It's good."

"Better than homemade protein balls?"

"Let's say I've broadened my horizons both by choice and demands close to blackmail."

"Getting our money's worth, huh?"

"I do owe Hud 737 dollars."

"He hasn't forgotten."

I promise, buddy. I promise.

CHAPTER 15

Saturday, October 23, 2021

Drives have historically been significant connective times in our fifteen years together. Good or bad, there's something therapeutic about a long road trip talk. Maybe it's the boredom, maybe it's the forced togetherness, or maybe it's just easier to talk to someone without having to look them in the eye. Whatever it may be, the open road always gives us time to solve the world's problems and dream about the one-day events that are now in question.

This was not one of those car rides.

Silence is a currency that is used wisely in my world, and the whole way up I-85, I went all in. I saw Michael shift from time to time, and when he did, I caught his eyes darting quickly to my side of the truck to assess my mood.

Now, we're heading up 278, almost in North Carolina, and neither of us has said a single word *still*. I usually have two reasons why I shut down and refrain from speaking: either I'm beyond pissed or I have no clue what to say. Today it's *both*.

The windows are cracked as we cross the state line, and I can already smell the damp sourwood trees. The scent closes around me like after a summer rain that transforms the pavement into dreamy steam. I closed my eyes and let the wind wash over my face until I felt the fresh air in the bottom of my lungs. It's going to be hard to stay mad while I'm intoxicated by the mountains. It reminds me of when I was a kid and I was upset. My dad would always chant, "Don't smile, Ruby. Don't you smile!" and it got me every time. My face would crack into a grin and then a full-fledged toothless smile. Was that a sweet way to change the tone, or was it manipulation to stop a kid from pouting?

Shit.

I'm not going to do that to Hudson and Nali anymore.

Michael is the first to break the silence. "The air up here is amazing, huh?" His window is cracked too, and I feel his body relaxing as we get closer and closer to the property.

"It is," I state, feeling vulnerable, and I focus on the pine trees passing rhythmically with a *whoosh, whoosh, whoosh.*

"I'm going to stop by Forks of the River to get some supplies for the night. Can you grab whatever you want to snack on and drink?" he asked.

I started to panic. "We can't take food to the property! What about the bears?" I think about being a bear burrito in my Eno, and chills run up my spine.

"The bears are hibernating. We'll be fine!" He said it, but I know he's not convinced of his own reassurance.

The playlist gods strike again, and Chris Stapleton's "Starting Over" comes on and fills the silence between us in the mountain air that's rushing through the cab. I turn to look at him, and it seems he had the same idea. He has on the "free gift" glasses from the daddy-daughter dance at the elementary school two years ago. Nali Blue *still* talks about that night. Although they are cheap as hell, I think they look hot on him. They remind me of simpler times, when the sand, the sun, the mountains, the rivers called, and we answered. If the question was, "Should we go?" the answer was always, "*Why not?*"

Now to plan a weekend trip, it takes securing all, and I mean all, of the following: work, kids, cats, bills, sports, food, medicine, bank account, and sanity. And when those all align, we call that a miracle.

Funny how the risk of losing your wife will make you figure out how to align these factors a little more strategically.

I see a few gray hairs sparkle in the dropping sunlight on the side of Michael's head. I've said it before, but I'll say it again: Michael's sexy. "Is there a food truck at the taproom tonight? We could eat there before we go to Sweetleaf?" I looked away, trying to avoid the next sentence that I knew was going to come out of his mouth.

"Rubes, are you…scared?" he teased, and I took the bait to hear him laugh.

"Hell, yeah, I'm scared! And you should be too! If a bear comes after us, I can run farther than you!" I push his shoulder as he belly laughs.

"Oh my gawd, Rubes, you know you don't have to have endurance. You've gotta have *speed,* love. And *you know* I have you beat there." He bounces and shakes his shoulders in a vain attempt to dance, and I shake my head at his goofy grin.

Being dramatic, I say, "You really might be the *worst* man alive if you pushed me aside and sprinted past me to evade the damn bear. I mean, I really feel safe now going into the woods with you! Do we even have service to ping our location? I have to tell Charleigh where to look if I go missing."

"You listen to *Crime Junkies* too much," he states, and he's not wrong.

Shout-out to Ashley and Brit!

"And?" I interject as I snap a selfie with the passing road sign. I open up the message thread that's consistently checked by my sisters and send out the evidence.

> *Just so you know what I'm wearing. Heading to camp at Sweetleaf with Michael...there may be bears. And he's faster than me. Pray.*

"I just sent Charleigh and Naomi the itinerary, as well as an updated photo to show the cops. Don't try me or my sisters."

He lets out a guffaw that hits my soul. "Oh, Ruby, I missed you."

I offer a quick smile, but I don't confess.

I missed you too.

It's funny how almost losing everything you've worked for makes a week feel like an eternity. As Shakespeare once wrote, "Sad hours seem long."

"Well, we're almost there, so why don't you order our food from whatever truck they have there tonight, and I'll go get us a drink after I go into the outfitter to get a few supplies," he suggests, and I'm not mad at the plan.

Cocktails and food trucks are my favorite combo.

The car crackles and pops into the gravel parking lot, and the place is busy tonight. Saturday on a cool fall night in Rosman? Can't get better than that. As I step out of the truck, I feel the instant shift of energy. Gone are the honking cars and loud backfires. Gone are the never-ending responsibilities of the house that loom over any relaxing opportunities at home. This is the first time we have been here since being the actual landowners, and I noticed that I walk a little taller through the gravel and to The Lunchbox truck. It makes me smile.

Michael's fingers brush mine as we walk lockstep up the stone steps to the courtyard. I feel the shock of electricity as we touch, and I don't pull away.

A man strummed his banjo with his companion at the table directly behind the truck, and I recognized the blue-grass tune as he closed his eyes and sang softly and proudly.

I love how bluegrass singers can do that.

Another group of fishermen were packing up their gear for the evening, and a few little kiddos were chasing a sweet mutt puppy in circles until they all collapsed on the grass in laughter and bark fits. Their parents watched in familiar relief as the puppy was doing a fantastic job of wearing them out before bed. My heart suddenly aches for my own kids, and I wish they could be here to pet the pup. I know they are in their own form of Disneyland staying with Mimi and Papa, so I don't allow myself to dwell on it too long. I'm so grateful they get to grow up with their grandparents right down the road.

"See ya in a sec?" Michael mouths, and I nod. He squeezed my fingers gently, and it made me feel safe.

Can I trust it?

Who knows, but it's a good feeling, nonetheless.

I scan the menu, and it is basically anything fried and all the things delicious, and my mouth begins to tingle with anticipation of the idea of each choice as I read down the list: pulled pork sandwich, corn dog, foot long, gyro, grilled chicken, fried chicken, and your choice of onion rings, fried pickles, coleslaw or french fries.

Funny, I was today years old when I found out that, in fact, it is not cold slaw but coleslaw.

I feel duped.

It's my turn to order, and the woman in the window yells, "What'cha havin', honey?"

Mountain people are my favorite. "Yes, ma'am, I'll take an order of the grilled chicken with fried pickles and a pulled pork sandwich with fries."

"All righty. What kind of sauce do you want with that chicken, hun?" she asked without missing a beat on the computer screen where she pecked in the order.

"None, thank you." I almost confessed to having Chick-fil-A sauce in my handbag, but I refrained.

If you know, you know.

"All right, your number is 22. I'll yell it out when it's ready, and you just come pick it up right yonder." She pointed at the pickup window, and I thanked her as I turned to find a table. Twenty-two—our family's number. My dad's father died on March 22, 2007, and ever since, the number 22 has shown up over and over again, and we always take it as a sign that Boom-pa's in it. He used to call me when I was in college and yell into the receiver, "Ruby, ya married yet?" I would always answer, "No, but you can find me one!" and he would reply, "I'll go pick you up one on 278!" and look at me now...on 278 (literally) eating dinner with my husband and the number is...

"Twenty-two!" yelled the woman in the window, and it shook me from my trance. I was about to stand up to go get it, but Michael grabbed the baskets with his spare hand and delicately walked over to me with food, drinks, and a grocery bag that seemed to be full of goodies. He knows the way to my heart.

"Look at you showing off! How did you know that was our order?" I ask as I help distribute the food and drink between us.

He pops a fry into his mouth and casually states, "I knew it had to be ours. It was order 22." He points up to the sky where the sun is fading in the west as an orangey pink transforms the clouds that seem to burst from the peaks. The foliage is in full force, and the golden streaks that the sun paints perfectly on Round Mountain are giving me life. "Thanks, Boom-pa!" he claims, and he takes a ginormous bite of his sandwich.

"No way," I challenge, and he confesses.

"You're right," he concedes as he picks up the plastic table marker. "I saw this and wanted to mess with you. Still cool that we got 22. I'll take it as Boom-pa approves of this trip." It actually melts my heart that he says this, and I nod as I dig through my hand bag to find the sauce. "No, don't tell me you brought your own sauce,." He had a mouthful of pork, and it made me giggle.

"So what? I like Chick-fil-A sauce, okay?" I pick up a pickle and dip it in the newly opened packet that I finally found in my purse.

"I love you, Big Mama." He grinned as he continued to wolf down his sandwich.

"Shut up," I tease. "You're eating like someone is going to take it from you! Why so fast?"

"I want to get to the property before dark so we can set up with some natural light left in the sky." We work at finishing our baskets and leave a good tip for The Lunchbox until next time. Michael grabs the bag of supplies, and I make him promise there is no food in its contents. He promises, and we head to the truck for our final stop: Sweetleaf.

Dusk has taken over, and as we hike down the old logging road to our property, I look both left, right, and behind me, constantly trying to intimidate any bears away with my intense stare. Somehow, I don't think it'll work, so I try to nonchalantly walk closer to Michael, but I'm caught.

"Nervous, Big Mama?" I didn't look, but I already know the goofy grin he is sporting like he always does when I admit that I'm scared and look to him for protection. It must be something set deep in the makeup of masculinity. Right now, I don't give a shit. I don't want to be Round Mountain's midnight drive-through serving the Saturday special of Ruby Blue Burrito for the hungry bears.

If I get eaten, spread my crystal collection in rivers where kids look for rocks.

It's in my will.

"Zip it, Michael. I'm trying to visualize the bears going far, far from our property." I grab his arm as I trip over a root, and he steadies me easily even with the lantern in his hand.

"Careful, Rubes. I don't want to have to carry you out of here." He looked at me with a wink and then kept trekking forward. Sweetleaf Falls is a quarter mile into the woods from the road, and I can hear it before it comes into view. We reach it as the sun's glow completely disappears, but the moving water sparkles in the dusk. It's so interesting to me how the light that was shining for the last twelve hours is just *gone*. I know the science behind it, but it's the unknown behind the weaving together of the universe that keeps me up at night sometimes. I looked up, but I was not ready for the blurred white magic of the Milky Way. I allowed my eyes to travel the panorama of the sky, and I stopped in my tracks.

"I've never seen it at night," I gasp. "It's unbelievable."

Michael had stopped with me. "Yeah, I'm kinda speechless."

It was phenomenal. It's the kind of sky that if you look at it for more than five minutes, God will bless you with a shooting star. To me, shooting stars are the red carpet of wish travel. If you see one and wish on it, your desires are put on display for all the heavens. I guess that would make throwing pennies in fountains the general admission of wishes. It reminds me of the groundlings of Shakespeare's time. They were very poor, and the one-cent admission got them into the smooshed standing-room-only dirt pit in front of the stage with a chance of getting a glimpse of the play. I guess you get what you get for a penny.

Whether it was a shooting star or a penny, I'll take the opportunity to let my wishes into existence anytime! I close my eyes, take a breath, and the next thought that pops into my mind surprises me.

I wish for peace.

Peace—that has been such a foreign word to me since I can remember. Looking back, the night watching my parents embrace in the storm was the last time I felt peace.

It's interesting, actually. I was so used to chaos that controlled my brain constantly that when I did have experience the joy of peace, I did something to flub it up almost immediately. I never trusted peace. If I had peace, it was only so some unforeseen power could rip it from my grasp and leave me feeling emptier than before because I actually got to experience the bliss that comes with serenity. I was a serial sabotager, and I hurt many people along my journey.

For that, I'm sorry.

I hope they know that.

But the past few months, I have experienced true, authentic, earned peace. This situation has put a dent in my armor, but I'll be damned if I'm gonna sit back and allow the blows to hit my skin. I've learned to fight for what means the most in this life because who knows if it's the only one I will get or not. I believe in my soul that I'm meant to thrive, not survive, and although it's not been easy, I have stood my ground and demanded for better from myself.

"I saw that." Michael snapped me back to Sweetleaf with his booming voice.

"Saw what?" I play coy.

"What'd you wish for?" His curious grin turned into a desperate one.

"Peace," I said plainly.

"You can't tell me," he joked, "then the wish won't come true!"

"I'm not scared. I know how to protect my peace. It's just nice to speak it into the universe every now and again. Helps with the manifestation process."

He says what I thought, "All right, Jade Brooks!" We both laugh.

"I'm honored to be like her. My mom's magical."

I'm who I am because of her unique view of the world alongside her strength as a woman who never settles for less than she deserves.

"As you should be," he agreed, and we continued the last few feet to the water's edge.

Everything about Sweetleaf Falls makes all the years of financial struggles worth it. I truly never thought the day would come when we would have our own slice of heaven in the mountains, but here we are, and it's unreal.

The moon dances on the surface of the stream, and it perfectly highlights the ebb and flow of one of nature's greatest resources. The water is mountain runoff from the French Broad River, and it's cold year-round. I lean down and immerse my fingertips in the ever-moving current. As my hand churns the surface, the water hurries to find a way around it as if it were telling me that there's no time to waste, but it hugs me before it moves on to its next destination downstream. When I'm here, nature speaks to me. The water cleanses my thoughts, the moon recharges my soul, and the rhododendrons surround the property to create a sense of protection and love. The mist from the falls creates droplets on my eyelashes, and it accumulates until a drop succumbs to gravity, and I see it join its fellow friends in the creek.

I hear Michael clear his throat, and I turn to see him watching me. "You're beautiful, Rubes. It always amazes me how beautiful you truly are." He grins, and I look into his eyes without turning away. "I'm going to get the fire started." He leaves me with my thoughts and the water. I lie on the dry, cold rock that forms the second tier of the falls and look up at the sky. It's dark now, and the air is thinning by the minute. I wrap my vest tightly around my core and allow my mind to wander.

I think back to February 2016. Just the mention of that year can make my heart drop and my stomach flip. That's the year I almost gave up on life. I almost allowed my eating disorder to completely take over and rob me of my existence. My body and my mind were possessed, and there seemed to be no way out. I look over and see Michael chopping wood to put on the smoldering kindling. He never gave up on me even when I gave up on myself. His support saved me. I borrowed his want and will for me to live when I didn't see the value in my own existence. I'm thankful for him. I don't need him to understand my worth anymore. I feel that on my own. I do need him, though. He is my person, and I can't imagine doing life with anyone else.

With a loud crack of the axe, I see the last piece of wood go flying, and he wipes the sweat from his brow and states, "All right, we are ready for the hammocks. Can you give me a hand?"

"Sure." I slowly rise from the rock and head to the packs. I retrieve the two Enos, the ropes, and the carabiners and begin working to secure them to the trees. Michael silently joins me, and we begin working on the setup together. His biceps bulge through his North Face pullover, and I'm distracted by his hands once again. He tugs on the ropes to test the strength, and he jumps in the hammock in one swift motion, surprisingly smoothly, and pats my hammock that is hanging centimeters from his.

"Join me." His invite sends electricity down my spine, and the goose bumps come without warning.

I cautiously move toward the hanging cloth. I'm a total klutz, and I cannot afford another fall at any height, so I open the folded material carefully and contemplate the best plan of action. I commit, put one leg in while holding it open, and then shakily lift the other leg to follow. The hammock shifts back and forth at an alarming rate, and I let out a squeal of both excitement and fear. I feel Michael's hand steady the Eno, and I slip in and melt into the cocoon and relax my body. I can feel Michael's body resting against mine, but the thin layer of nylon taffeta separating us takes me back to the innocent days of touching through layers, and it makes my body ache for his embrace. I sit in the feeling instead of acting on it. Some moments are for action, and some moments are for being still. At this moment, I just want to feel the safety of hanging next to the man I love.

"Pretty comfortable, huh?" He puts his hands behind his head and crosses his feet on the taut ropes. I hear the fire crackle, and the moon is beginning to peak over Round Mountain in the distance.

"Surprisingly, yes!" I answer, and I feel his hand slip over the barrier that separates us, and he laces his fingers through mine.

"I truly love you, Rubes. I hate that I broke your trust, but we'll work this out. I can't lose you and the kids." I hear him swallow hard as he stares at the stars above.

"I know." I squeeze his hand and look up too. "Do you remember the day you dropped me off at Manna House?"

"The best and worst day of my life," he states plainly. "It's hard to forget that."

"Why did you not leave me then? I deserved it."

"You're my girl, Rubes. It was just never an option." He said it with a finality that made me realize he had come to this conclusion long ago, no matter his mistakes.

"Why?" I ask, and I mean it. "Why is it not an option?"

"Because like you always tell me, God, the universe, or whatever you want to call it works together to conspire all that we want and need. All we have to do is make space for it. I chose you back in 2007, and no bump in the road will derail that."

"Was it hard to stay and fight?" My eyes narrow, and my lips purse. I asked the question, but I already know the answer.

"Hell, yeah, it was so hard. It killed me to watch you get ED faced and completely shut down or break down. You wouldn't eat, Rubes! I watched you fade away more and more, and I was terrified that one day, you would just not wake up. I used to hold my fingers under your nose in the middle of the night to make sure you were still breathing. I just knew that one time I would check, and you would be gone."

"I'm sorry."

"There's nothing to be sorry for, babe. Your eating disorder was out of your control, but you chose to get help. *That's* what made me stay. I knew that the Jade Brooks in you wouldn't allow you to accept defeat, so I took a step back, gave you space to heal, and waited for the light to come back into your eyes." He turned to look at me. "And see"—he touched my cheek—"there it is!"

Tears welled up and threatened to overflow. Words would not form, so I offered a smile as I leaned into his palm. He held me firmly, his intense gaze breaking my walls down, and I needed to be held. Our hammocks hung side by side, but that wasn't enough for me. I shifted my weight toward him, and he understood my intent. He opened the side of his hammock closest to me, slid his arm under my torso, and made my transition a fluid one with his strength. I nestled my head on his chest and listened to his heartbeat echo. He stroked my hair gently, and I closed my eyes.

"I'm sorry I let the distance between us grow so big that you felt you had to look elsewhere for connection," I confessed, and his hand stopped.

"Ruby, nothing you did caused me to make the dumbass choice I did. That's on me. I should have fought for us instead of looking for an easy fix. Nothing worth having comes easy, and I never intend on dropping the ball in our marriage again." He pauses. "I fucked up, Rubes. I hurt you, Camryn, the kids. It's something I can't take back, but I sure as hell can make the necessary changes moving forward."

"What does that mean?" I ask, and I truly want to know the answer. I have never been tempted to cheat on him, so this is all Greek to me.

"It means that I have to get help in the areas I'm broken. It means that I need to start my day in prayer and end it in prayer. It means that it's my turn to fix *me*. I hyperfocused on you and your healing for so long. I put myself, my feelings, my struggles to the side, and it finally caught up to me. I have an appointment with a counselor named Ronnie on Monday. He was recommended by the church." He pauses.

"You called Trey?" I asked, and he nodded. Trey is our pastor, and although we have not attended church since the world shut down in 2020, we still stay connected. Church is not a necessity for me. I feel a strong, primal connection to God and the universe that is not defined by four walls and hymns, but Michael craves the community that church provides. I'm learning that he needs to have accountability to stay on track, and that is more than okay. "Wow, I'm glad you reached out."

"Yeah, he was supersupportive. Anyways, I'm no good at all this, but I plan to become better. Ronnie and I are going to focus on getting back to the core of my relationship with Christ so I can become the best version of myself for me and our family." His hand was stroking my hair again, and even out in the middle of the dark woods, I don't think I have ever felt more safe. His lips pressed against the crown of my head, and I sunk deeper into his embrace. "We're gonna make it, Ruby Blue. I'll do everything in my power to make sure of it."

"Me too."

I allowed myself to close my eyes and drift to sleep with the crackling fire, the running of the falls, and the up-and-down rise and fall of Michael's relaxed breathing. It seemed to be the beginning of a new chapter in the story of our journey through this life together, and I'm beyond grateful to be doing it together.

"*Happiness is only real when shared*" (Chris McCandless).

CHAPTER 16

Sunday, April 3, 2016

I give a slight *tap, tap* on the door to Dr. Leslie's office, and I hear the familiar, "Come in, Ruby!" and I push open the door with a creek. My mood coming into this meeting today is exactly what I expected: terrified.

"Hey there! Come have a seat." Dr. Leslie patted the chair across from her, and I reluctantly complied. This room still gives me first-day flashbacks. The day I got here, there was a tornado watch, and this office is the only interior room on the ground floor, so that's where I was introduced to my fifteen new friends.

That day the storm caught me.

The watch turned into a warning before I could even sign the paperwork to be admitted, and I was rushed to the safe closet-sized room with all the other girls who were finishing up the afternoon "challenge snack" that consisted of taste testing chocolate to see if they had a preference for the different samples. Here I was, anxious as all get out about this whole damn hospitalized-treatment thing and claustrophobic me, who hasn't allowed herself to eat real chocolate in years, is offered a plateful of goodies by a sarcastic nurse saying it's not optional when I say, "Thank you, ma'am, but no thank you, ma'am," and then the screaming, crying blond bombshell, who came in just before me, is acting exactly how I feel, and now they are telling us to duck and cover. Lord, take me now.

It was a memorable entrance to treatment, to say the least.

"How are you feeling about today?" she asked, and I was reminded of the inevitable.

"Nervous." I let the one word escape, but I'm afraid if I have to go into more than one-word answers, I will lose it.

"Understandably," Dr. Leslie says, and she folds her hands on her lap properly. She was probably only fifteen years older than me, but she was a classy lady. She reminded me of my gran. "So let's do a final check-in so you can get the heck out of here, huh?" She smiles, and I know it's not a choice, but she's not steered me wrong yet. Suddenly, I feel sad for my other counselors who don't get to be in this moment even though they helped me pave the way to get here. I wiped a tear that snuck out of line, and she asked, "Where did that come from?"

"I wish they could be here." I sniff and grab the tissue box.

Crying forty-five seconds in—new record.

"Who's they?"

"All the counselors before you that helped me get here." Tears were flowing, and I dabbed them with the tissue. I think of Dr. Sapphire and Dr. Parsons. Without them, I may not be alive.

"Oh, Ruby, you really are a gem. They *are* here, Love. They were always here." Her soft eyes feel so authentic, and I trust her deeply. "Think about it like this: you are a teacher. How many kids have you taught over the years?"

"Kicking me out and making me do math today? You're servin' an extra level of cruelty!" We both laugh, and I start attempting the math. "Okay, so nine years of teaching. I teach roughly one hundred forty kids a year, multiplying, rounding, um."

"Around twelve hundred kids." She saves me.

"Yes, if you say so."

"So you have taught over twelve hundred students, and that's not counting the kids you coached, so we'll round up to fifteen hundred. That's approximately fifteen hundred kids you have impacted over the years. Even if you are not there for the milestones—the graduations, the weddings, the babies—you're still *there.* Each person you impact in this world carries you with them in their mind, their views, their beliefs, and forever and always, you're a part of them."

I let the weight of her statement set in, and the sadness I felt melted to joy.

"It's the truth. Now, for my activity. Ready?"

"Maybe?" I lift my eyebrows, and she matches my rediscovered sass.

"All right, then here we go." She wiggled in her chair to get more comfortable, and her pen was ready to react when commanded. "We focused a lot in the beginning of your time here on your relationship with your mom and dad and their role in your childhood. How have you grown in your views of your time growing up since coming to the Manna House?."

"I feel like I can see my parents and their role in my eating disorder downfall more truthfully now." It feels good to say it aloud.

"Explain that."

"Well, I've learned that I suffered horribly from anxiety long before it was a buzzword. I used to be so angry at my mom and dad for not *doing* anything to help me, but I realize now that they were doing the best they could with what they had at the time. When my dad came to visit, he told me that one doctor even told them to ignore my fear of food and eating because addressing it will just make the problem worse." I took a deep breath. "And I've forgiven them for the turbulence I experienced in my formative years. Although they're not perfect, they never gave up on me. That has to count for something, right? They brought me into this world, stuck with parenting even when it sucked, and they continue to love and support me through it all. I only have one life as their daughter, and I truly can't imagine wasting one more minute on the past when I can shape a new future."

I no longer blame them for the wolves.

"That's powerful, Ruby."

"It feels powerful." I surprised myself with that answer.

"Good for you. Now, what about Michael and the kids? What are you taking away from a mother-and-wife lens?"

My stomach drops.

"It's still hard to forgive myself for the things I've done or neglected in the past, but I know dwelling in that guilt isn't productive." A flashback of the last night I was at home floods my brain. Michael and I were arguing about going to treatment, and he set boundaries that I wasn't expecting him to enforce.

"Ruby, you're dying! You're actually dying. Do you want to be alive to see our kids grow up? Do you really want them to be left without a mom? I can't do this for you, Rubes. I can't. It's killing me watching you slowly *kill yourself.*"

He gave me an ultimatum: accept help or he would be gone. I remember the feeling on the rough almost-sandpaper carpet on my cheek as I collapsed to my knees, and my head fell to the ground in agony. It's like the eating disorder realized its host was evicting it, and it held on for dear life. That night, I used every behavior I had ever known. If my ED was going to get the boot, it was gonna put up a fight, a last ditch effort to take control, but it didn't work. The next day, I was in Dr. Sapphire's office with my white flag in tow.

"Yeah, it will take time, but remember what you need to focus on. All the work you've done to heal yourself will directly affect their experience in life. With a healed mama, they can have the opportunity to have a healthy role model to guide them through their journey in this life. They'll face struggles. However, now they'll have a mother to guide them through the trenches, not one that helps dig them."

"I have to continue to look at it from that perspective, but it's still hard to shake the memories."

"That's because you haven't made new ones yet. Just imagine all the beautiful new memories you're about to create to replace the bad ones. You have a second chance at life, Ruby. What you've done here is a big deal, and no one can take that from you." She gently grabs my hand and squeezes it. It reminds me of dinner table prayers with their little hands in mine. I always squeeze when we say amen.

"I'll have to trust you on this one," I offer, and she winks and moves on.

"Honestly, one of the most memorable moments I watched you overcome was facing your unhealed beliefs and feelings about your first love, Marco. I can honestly say, I've never had a client chuck Sprite cans at a picture on a rock before!" We both laugh.

"You know, I blamed Marco for my eating disorder for so long, but none of it was his fault. I almost wish I could go back and be the person I am now so he could have experienced the true me, not the manic me." I confess this, and the tears come instantly.

"Could a sixteen-year-old boy that may have been disordered himself due to all the same factors you experienced

239

actually appreciate any woman, much less a confused sixteen-year-old girl trying to figure out her place in the world? No one but you expects you to be flawless, Ruby Blue."

"You're right, but I'm no longer angry at him. I only hope he has the peace in his life that every human deserves."

"This way of thinking will only serve you and your family well in the long run. You'll see."

"Yeah, I get that now."

"How have you handled the exercise component? You spoke with Ann about it in one of your sessions with her. She told me that you and her discussed that, for now, it's best if you don't run for exercise. Do you think you'll be able to keep that up?"

"It's funny. When I was waking up at 4:00 a.m. to 'get a run in' before my day started, I remember thinking, 'Am I really gonna have to do this the rest of my life?' I truly thought it was a sad existence. I just didn't know how to stop. I wouldn't have if I hadn't come here. I feel ashamed that I wasted so much time, energy, and sanity over running. The worst part, I missed waking my kids up and taking them to school for two years. *Two years*. For what? To get my mile time down to subsix minutes at thirty-one? Who even cares how fast I can run a mile?"

"Do you care?" she asks, and it's a fair question.

"Hell no. I've learned something about myself here. I have a disconnect in giving myself credit for what I have accomplished when it's over and done. For example, I thought that if I was going to be a marathon runner, I had to *always* be one for it to *count*."

"What do you mean by count?" she prods, and I'm ready to answer.

"There's a part of me that truly thought that if I'm not *currently* doing something, it never happened. I know it sounds crazy, and it is, but I'm so thankful that I can finally look back on the things I've done, accomplished, and worked for and not only give myself credit but also allow myself to move on without feeling like I gave up or failed. It's okay for my plans, life, and goals to shift over time. That's why we have seasons in life. Everything is temporary, and moving on from a season is not a failure. It's growth. Does that make sense?"

"Absolutely. That's a beautiful lesson. How does it connect to running for you?"

"Yes, I was a runner. Yes, I was good. Yes, I worked hard. And yes, it went too far. But instead of continuing the cycle of shame and regret, I'm going to give myself grace, thank my body for all the miles, and shift into a more balanced relationship with exercise and body acceptance. I ran to numb out. I've learned that feeling isn't a bad thing. It's actually a blessing. I'm ready to slow down and experience my life instead of running from it."

It feels amazing to speak those words and actually believe them.

"Beautiful. Lastly, what have you learned about your relationship with food?"

"Oh, man, this one is big. The time I've spent with Ann learning about the science behind our bodies and their relationship with food and its actual *need* for it has truly changed my perspective of how I view eating. I never realized or wanted to realize the damage I was doing to my organs and mind for so long. I think everyone should have to see a dietitian in their life to debunk all the toxic myths that we are conditioned to believe."

"Yes, it's a crime how we are coerced by society to hate ourselves so someone can make a dollar." She shakes her head in disgust, and I agree completely.

"Right? It makes me so sad. *Ugh.* I've also learned it's okay to *enjoy* food. I think it was a combination of growing up in the '90s when the government and media attacked fat and sugar and family history of ED behaviors to cope that made me ashamed to admit that I love to eat."

"Amen, sister!" Dr. Leslie gave me a cheesy high five, but it made me smile.

"I'm not sure how long I have or what actually happens when this physical life is over, but I know this: I'm *done* wasting the precious time I have on this earth."

"Wow. Tell me more about not wasting precious time."

"You see, when I was in my disorder, I had no room to *think.* My brain was on a constant replay of self-deprecating thoughts and catastrophizing the narrative, so I went through life on autopilot. You know the old saying, '*Lights are on, but no one's home*'? That was me. I didn't believe that was me until I watched the beautiful women here at Manna House get the same blank stare that Michael described in me. I don't ever want to miss out on the beauty of life by holding on to the armor I created as a defenseless child that I no longer need as a knowing adult."

"An eating disorder as armor?"

"Ha! I'm getting my whole money's worth now. I haven't told anyone about this since a lightning storm in 1991."

"I'm honored."

"When I was about six or seven, I imagined that terrifying wolves would pace my room at night. I didn't trust that they were in my imagination because they seemed *so* real. When I finally accepted they were just a part of my anxious brain, it's like I unlocked the door for them to take up permanent residency. Over time, they morphed into more realistic fears solicited by unrealistic expectations. It was so gradual that I really can't recall when and where I noticed their complaints and demands, but I remember following them. I allowed the wolves to dictate my mood, my tone, my agenda, and because of that, I missed so much. It's like the kid at the concert that can't put the phone down to enjoy the moment. That was me. I was that kid, so wrapped up in my own brain that I couldn't see two inches in front of my own nose, and those are years I'll never get back."

Dr. Leslie reaches for a tissue.

"I'm done with the wolves," I sniff. "I want to let go of the crutches that no longer help me along my path in life. I have no need for them anymore."

I lean forward.

"I want to meet the real me, the real Ruby Blue, you know?"

"Congratulations, Ruby Blue. I believe you're well on your way."

I take a breath and let it out slowly.

"I'm ready to let go of the shame and guilt and live in my truth."

"What truth is that?"

"The truth that *I'm enough*. That feels too simple, but I can't seem to form the words to do it justice. Treatment's taught me that I have permission to be a human, medication is a tool that's a gift not a sin, and I'm pretty fucking badass for stepping in the ring to fight my demons head on."

"Amen." Dr. Leslie clasps her hands over mine. "Ruby, you're a special one. You're gonna help a lot of people in this world. I just know it."

"I'm just thankful I helped myself. I deserve to be *free*."

"Yes, you do."

No more huff and puff, wolves.

No more.

CHAPTER 17

Sunday, May 29, 2022

"Will that be all, ma'am?"

"Yes, sir! Thank you!" I grab the off-brand meat stick and Cherry Coke Zero with a smile, and I put on my Ray-Bans as the classic *ting* of the gas station door announces my departure. The school's-out sun hits differently, and I can almost imagine all the other teachers breathing the same sigh of *we-made-it* relief as we trade our dry-erase markers and side-eyes for cocktails, coffee, and sleeping in.

Anyone who knows the ridiculous amount of energy and work it takes to run a classroom daily applauds us as we hit the exits and sprint to our summer break. However, there are those out there who turn a nose up at the "paid time off." News flash: teachers only get paid for the days they work, and it's those same individuals who are at open house shoving little Johnny at us with desperate eyes, thankful that the professionals are almost in charge again. I say that as a mother myself. I love Nali and Hud, but if 2020 taught us anything, it's that teachers are essential to parents not eating their young.

I think about my students whom I'll no longer see in the hallways come this fall, and it makes me smile in both sadness and love. My kids this year were special. I'm not sure how I would've made it out of this fall without them. They unknowingly taught me that I have all the tools and more than enough strength to make it through any obstacle that life throws my way. If I didn't have their youth, their hope, and their innocence to push me to get out of bed to be their teacher, I'm not sure I would've bothered getting out of bed at all. They'll never know how each hug, each hello, each inter-action was the omen and energy I needed to continue. And simultaneously, it was also their strength to face hard things that gave me the confidence to leave. So here I am, heading up Highway 11, eating my jerky and sippin' my Coke with the windows down. My car's packed to the brim, Panda and Murphie are in the front seat sleeping in the sun, and Nali and Hud, with their hands hanging out the windows, are singing "Glorious" with their hair blowing in the wind.

"Mama, toss me the Funyuns!" Hudson called, and I handed them back.

"Do you have my SmartPop?" Nali was cracking open her can of Coke.

"Right here." I twist my arm to unimaginable positions to get around the boxes, and I feel like a kid trying to steal a bag of chips from a vending machine.

"Thanks, Mama," Nali smiles.

"Yeah, Mama, thank you. How far are we from Rosman?"

"About twenty minutes." I can smell the sourwood already.

I look back at my children, and I know that every deci-sion I've ever made since the day I left Manna House has been with them in the forefront of my mind. And to prove that, we're going to Sweetleaf to camp for the summer, but it won't be our forever home. Yes, I wanted to be surrounded by the safety of the rhododendrons, cleansed by the Sweetleaf Falls mist while I drink my morning coffee, and fulfilled with nature and life all around me. But it's not what's best for my heart and my soul back there—not yet, at least. One day, we will have golden-hour walks and starry-night fires, but now, family first.

I decided to move to a small lake town with Charleigh and Robert and their three blond boys just down the road. They've been there for three years, and they love it. Dad and Pat are buying a house only four doors down, so there will be a lot of "can I go to Papa and Mimi's?" in my near future. But you can't beat it—family, slower lifestyle, less crowded, all with plenty of nature to be experienced. The moving water of Sweetleaf will still flood my dreams, but one can do worse than own a lake house and a mountain haven.

"Mama, play 'Wonderwall,'" Nali asks, and I am more than happy to comply. They got their taste in music from me. My whole family can recite every song on my playlist. When I hear them humming Dave or Tom Petty as they do their homework or pal around the yard, my heart smiles. The shuffle goes from Oasis, to Swift, to Petty, and then back to Nicks. I could drive for hours listening to the soundtrack of my life.

"*Today is gonna be the day they were gonna throw it back to you. By now you should've somehow realized what you've got to do.*" Both kids are singing along. "*I don't believe that anybody feels the way I do about you now.*" My smile can't be missed. This is exactly what I wanted. This is exactly what we need. Spending the summer with the kids in Western North Carolina is a dream come true. but it's also bittersweet, for sure.

I held a retirement party for my wolves last week. Yeah, I figured thirty-eight years of petrol deserves a nice extended vacation, huh? I think I had it rough as a teacher. Man, those wolves had a J-O-B dealing with my brain all these years. As I approach my forties, I'm in awe of the things that I used to dwell on or claim I knew as a twenty-something. I was talking with a random man in the line at the store yesterday, and he put it this way: "*If I were to run into myself at twenty-five, I'd knock the hell out of my pompous know-it-all ass.*" I laughed at the vision of this older man scolding his younger self, but it also made me think about what I would say to my younger self. The narrative that played out surprised me, and I think of it as I look in the rearview mirror now.

If I could talk to my younger self, I'd give her a huge hug, tell her that all she's going through will lead her to the place she's meant to be, and that her body is the least interesting thing about her. It's the old cliché saying: if I only knew then what I know now.

But I've grown past shaming my younger self for doing all I could to survive all those years. That's what my eating disorder was, my desperate attempt to survive my anxiety. Manna House, medication, and my will to live changed the trajectory of my life six years ago, and Regina Love was right. My willingness to fight for my freedom from my demons has made me the generational change that will allow me to help those two angels back there navigate their journey on this planet. I won't do it perfectly, but I will always show up. I used to think that I needed to do something great and grandiose with my recovery journey for it to be worth the time, money, and pain. But now, looking into their eyes makes me know that being their healthy, balanced mother is more than enough.

I see my amethyst hanging from my rearview mirror, and I have a peace that only comes from a deep place of satisfaction and self-love. The past year tried to break me, but I didn't let it. The Wailin' Jennys cover of "Wildflowers" fills the speakers, and I let the fresh air fill my lungs to capacity. I let out a long, slow breath as they sing, "*Run away. Go find a lover. Run away. Let your heart be your guide.*" The old Ruby would've done just that: run away. The old Ruby would've used Michael's mishap as an excuse to spiral, an excuse to give into the wolves and feed the beast, but I didn't. I stayed strong. I stayed true to myself.

I've learned over the years that I'm worth knowing, and not in an egotistical better-than-others way but in a way that each and every human is worth knowing. My unique view of the world, my empathetic soul, and my love for both humans and nature are gifts that I cherish, and those who get to experience life through my eyes will get a perspective that is rare and beautiful because it is *mine*. I wouldn't have this perspective without weathering all the storms, so instead of drowning in the past, I'm gonna dance in the rain.

I've always loved storms.

"We're almost there, guys!"

"Yes! I can feel the creek now." Hudson's head is out the window. His eyes are closed and his mouth open, as if to taste the sourwood in the air.

"I've got to finish my house for Tiny Tim!" Nali's referring to the sweet baby mouse we found while clearing our camping site last time we were here.

"Remember, nature's way is best, so if Tiny Tim is not where we left him, we'll just choose to believe he's moved on with his mouse life to bigger and better things!" I don't have the heart to be honest here, but she nods and accepts my innocent vision as truth, and all is well in Nali's heart.

We pull onto Sweetleaf Lane, and Dave's guitar fills my ears. The acoustic beginning perks all our ears up, and we begin to sing "You & Me" in unison. It's the song that Michael and I danced to at our wedding. I thought he chose a classic Frank Sinatra song, but when he held out his hand to take mine and Dave Matthews's love song about growing old together filled the room, I knew I made the right choice. I married my soul mate, and even if I'd known all we'd go through, I'd take his hand again and again.

The gravel pops and cracks as we pull onto the logging road that leads to our sacred spot, and I slowly approach my happy place with pride. This is what life's about. Connecting with nature and my family is all I want, and I've walked the line to make it here. I think of my favorite quote from Chris McCandless once more: *"Happiness is only real when shared."* He didn't get to live out his discovery, but I do, and I'm not going to waste one minute of my life doubting my worth anymore.

The car slows to a stop, and I can hear the falls in full force. Nali and Hud are out of the car in a flash, and I take a second to breathe in the last verse of the song: *"But right now, it's you and me forever, girl, and you know that we could be better than anything that we did. You know that you and me, we could do anything."* And then he appeared.

Adorned with a backward hat, baseball tee, Carhartts, and boots, Michael emerged from the rhododendrons with his axe in hand. I give him a grin, and he reciprocates with a smile. He slams the tool into the stump and walks to my open window and leans his elbows on the open pane.

"Glad you made it, Rubes."

"Me too. Need some help?"

"Heck, yeah. There's a ton of work to be done before we can set up camp."

"It'll be worth it. Anything worth having takes work."

"Amen."

He opens the car door, and I slip out into his embrace. He smells of wood and sweat, and I breathe in his energy once more before breaking away to look at him. You and I together, we can do anything. And here we are proving to ourselves that love is a choice, and we made the right one years and years ago, and we'll continue to fight for each other.

Until.

CHAPTER 18

Protect Your Peace
Letters from the Professionals

Letter from the author

Can we give Ruby Blue a round of applause? I mean, come on. I feel like this is a triumph that people would clap after, right? Ruby Blue is not just a character in a book. She's a part of anyone who has ever tackled their demons, a part of anyone who has faced their monsters, and a part of anyone who has wanted to give up but just freakin' *refused*. Her strength, her bravery, and her intentionality are a reminder that we all have the capability to overcome life-altering obstacles. Her humanity, her humility, and her humor are proof that we don't have to navigate them perfectly to be successful. Thank you for allowing me to share her with you all. It's been my honor.

I have often had people ask me how I knew I needed to get help with my disordered thoughts and behaviors, and one face immediately comes to mind. She was a young woman who was sharing her story of overcoming an eating disorder to a group of students, and I listened to her speak with my jaw literally on the floor. Her story was mine, yet I was calling my disordered lifestyle healthy, and she was calling her similar past a slow death. Her brave choice to share her experience with exercise addiction and anorexia led me to exploring my own actions and beliefs, which then took me to Genie Burnett at Manna. With her guidance, I began to navigate my own recovery journey, and I truly believe that sharing this book with you makes all the years of suffering worth it. You know why? If Ruby's story helps one person break free from the chains of addiction and disorder, then it was worth every claw and scratch it took to get to freedom.

To anyone who reads this book and relates in ways that you wish you didn't: just know you're not alone, and I encourage you to fight until you are free. It's worth it, love.

For those of you who realized something about your actions or beliefs toward your body and your health from Ruby's struggle, I pray you utilize the letters from my very own treatment team. I asked them to give you their perspective on why each avenue of treatment is necessary for long-term recovery, and their insight and knowledge are greatly appreciated.

Lastly, you are made of the same materials as the stars, and no matter how many lives you may have, *this one* is important enough to fight for. *You* are important enough to fight for. Find safety. Find love. And most importantly, find those things within *yourself.* You're not a burden. You're human. Search for yourself. Find yourself over and over and over again. And be kind to your inner child. They went through a lot to get you to where you are today.

When I say I love you, I mean it. Protect your peace. With everything you've got, protect your peace.

Much love,
Brooke

Letter from an eating disorder specialist

A Word to the reader:

This is a real-life, unadulterated, raw look at the inside of an individual with an eating disorder. This story is a combination of real and fiction. However, as the "character" playing Dr. Sapphire, I can let you know that the harsh reality portrayed in this book is real as it comes to the eating disorder clinician.

The eating disordered mindset is twisted, distorted, and in pain. The pain that the individual who has an eating disorder is excruciating. Sometimes it is because of a divorce, sometimes because of teasing by peers, and sometimes because of the hell-on-earth experiences that the individual goes through.

Treatment of an eating disorder is not for the novice. It is a daily, life and death battle. Every day, 23 people die from an eating disorder. That's roughly one per hour. You think you don't know anyone with an eating disorder? Think again. It could be your child's teacher, your boss, or your best friend. It could be you. Many times, people who struggle are "riding the line" between being thin and being nourished. Many individuals die of heart attacks, starvation, or suicide. Regardless, the struggle is real. The struggle is hard. The struggle can cause you to die.

This is why I was chosen to write this forward. I don't play with those with eating disorders. Why not? Too costly.

So if you think that you may have an eating disorder, disordered eating, or just simply have feelings of hate for yourself or your body, *please get help*. You have intrinsic value and worth. Please find a therapist or treatment center that knows what they are doing. There are many treatment centers in the United States that serve eating disorders. There are fewer places that treat trauma, and even fewer that treat both.

Oh, and treatment is *expensive*. Those that are fortunate to live in the US and have insurance with a major private company, you are fortunate. If you have Medicaid or Medicare, there are about 12-15 centers that can help you. If you do not have any form of insurance or have exhausted your insurance benefits, well, there are several organizations in the US that provide scholarships. They are fewer than the overwhelming need, but they are there. Manna Scholarship Fund is one of them.

I founded Manna in 2006. For 10 years, we raised 1.3 million and put 25 people in treatment. In 2016, I merged my private practice, Manna Treatment, with Manna Scholarship Fund, and have been able to expand the levels of care that we are able to provide. Now, we provide scholarships at all levels of care. We are based in Georgia and continue to provide scholarships in house, as well as across the US.

Manna is growing and will create the Manna House, which is a recovery residence for those in Partial Hospitalization, Intensive Outpatient, and Outpatient levels of care. We also have plans to open our own residential treatment program for women that need both eating disorder and trauma recovery treatment. As a nonprofit, we are able to build and create as fast as the donations come in. You can make a donation here: www.mannafund.org

Find a person and a place where you feel safe. It's out there. Help is available. You are worth it. If you don't believe me, ask someone that really knows you. They will tell you the same thing.

Let us know if we can help.

Genie Burnett, PsyD, CEDS-S.
CEO and clinical director
Manna Fund

Letter from a dietician

Dearest reader,

Contrary to what society might lead you to believe, our bodies are designed to thrive on a variety of nutrients. We need all of the following for our bodies to function properly: proteins, fats, carbs, water, vitamins, and minerals. They are all important and work together to fuel your body. A Registered Dietitian Nutritionist can educate you on their importance and what your individualized needs are because every single person is different. They may help you design a structured safe eating plan, teach about grocery shopping, meal preparation, navigating buffets or restaurant menus, adequate portioning, or work with you towards more intuitive eating concepts. Although a Dietitian's guidance is key to lasting balance, we know learning about the science of nutrition doesn't typically simply "turn off" an ED (eating disorder) brain or thoughts. Recovering from this disease takes the incorporation of a therapeutic approach, as well.

Like Ruby Blue's character models, having an awareness of your past experiences that potentially led to those first core thoughts or disordered eating behaviors is a necessary step in repairing your relationship with food.

Wait, what? What does that even mean?

Many times how we see or have programmed ourselves to respond to life can skew our rational cognitive thoughts which may lead to altered eating behaviors. Just as a friend may stay stuck in a relationship you know is not right or even harmful to them, an ED can keep us trapped in our ability to change our behaviors when it comes to choosing what, when, where, why, or how much to eat. Let's face it, breakups are tough. They can be painful and take working on ourselves to repair emotions, confidence, self worth and sometimes compassion to get back to our authentic selves.

Implementing and sustaining balanced nutrition behaviors to victoriously break up with ED with the help of a Nutrition Therapist on your treatment team is no different. Once we start to see food as something that can be amazingly supportive for our bodies, we can begin to clearly recognize how disordered eating behaviors were not serving us well in the past. This reflection is paramount to effectively fueling our bodies to promote recovery.

My prayer and hope for you is to have the strength to know you are valuable and worth this fight with each and every nourishing bite you choose to take. Let's do this!

Warm Regards,
Regina Saxton, RDN, LDN
www.reginasaxton.com

AUTHOR'S THANK-YOUS

I would first like to thank my mom and dad. I've always known they were special, and I think that's why I've always held them at such a high standard. I see my son do the same for me. Karma, huh? Glenn Malool and Nancy Blue are two of the most genuine, kind, loving, and giving people on the planet, and I'm blessed that it was my fate to be their daughter. Dad, you have always been there—always. Whether it was a flat tire six hours away or a play where I was cast as a not-so-honorable character, you were there. You've taught me what unconditional love is, and you've taught me how I want to love my own children. Thank you. Mom, I was tough on you, and I still am, but it's only because you're my favorite human on the planet. Your willingness to fight for your best life has paved the way for me to do the same for mine, and I can never thank you enough for that example you set for me. Ironically, the older I get, the more I turn into you, and the more I value that as one of my greatest accomplishments. I would not be who I am without you, and I'm pretty fucking amazing. I love you.

To my bonus parents Karen and Phil. Karen, at our first meeting when I was seven years old, I was skeptical. When you hiked your leg up and jumped up on that trampoline with us after the game, I was convinced: "this woman is awesome." Turns out, I wasn't wrong. You've always taken a back seat and accepted our crazy family dynamics, and it meant everything. You're my mom too and the one true gift that came from the divorce. Everyone agrees you're a saint, and there's a special place for you in heaven with all the shoes and wine you could ever want. I'll bring the cheese. And, Phil, you came in the middle of the story, somewhere around chapter 17 (lucky you!), but you didn't back down from my thwarts to derail your mission for love and happiness, and I couldn't be more grateful. You're exactly the man to challenge my mom while also loving her for the beautiful human she is. You're my favorite person to watch football with. You're always up for a project, a meal, or a drink, and I love that about you. Welcome to the family. We've only grown better with you becoming a part of it!

Now for my sisters—*deep breath*. Mandy, you've always been my rock. From letting me sleep with you when I was scared to holding my hand when I questioned everything, you've taken your big-sister role to heart, and an amazing heart is what you've got. I'm so excited to grow old watching lake sunsets and our kids connecting. You're my other half, and I love you. To Taylor, the music in my heart always leads me to you, and I see you believing that more and more. You completed our family, and I have loved watching you grow into the beautiful human that you are. I can honestly say you're my favorite person to just hang with because I can always just be myself and not feel I have to apologize for it. Thank you for growing with me. I can't wait to continue to do life and laugh with someone who gets me and likes pinot as much as me. Cheers.

To all the counselors, doctors, and staff who helped me find the want and will to heal, thank you. Your work matters. Your work is the reason I'm living today. Keep fighting for the one because each one of us matters.

To my best friend, thank you for learning how to live your best life alongside me. There's never been someone who has gotten me like you do. With you, I've learned how to have a real conversation without apology. I've had a sidekick to help me stand up when I fall (literally—the corner still doesn't make sense) and a voice of reason when it's time to step down. Our relationship is a connection and gift that I never expected to receive and something I never want to lose. I look forward to making time to "go to dinner" with you until the day I leave this earth. I love you.

To my students, past and present, I hope you cherish the words in this book. Each of you have helped me find them by sharing yourselves with me through my years as a teacher. I can't tell you how often you cross my mind, and I pray that you are living the life that you want and deserve. And if you're not, there's still time. Fight for that life you want until you're living it. Thank you for helping me write this book. I couldn't have done it without the years and years of you allowing me to practice telling my stories!

To my 2021–2022 students, where do I start? The world has just come out of a two-year pandemic, and I was so close to quitting teaching. I was looking for other jobs. I was even going to clean houses for a living because I lost all faith in my ability to continue to give and give and give one hundred percent of myself to the students daily, and I swore when that day came, I would quit. My husband helped convince me *to give it one more year. After year fifteen, we can reassess.* And then, August of 2021, you all walked through my doorway in F27 and flipped my world upside down. I only have so much space to write, but you know what magic happened in those four walls that year. Remember, read *The Alchemist* every ten years, and when you feel like giving up on anything that means something to you, read *The Four*

Agreements. Also, read these words and let them sink in: as freshmen in high school, you helped me achieve a dream I've had my whole life, and you also gave me the support and confidence to go for it. Don't let the names fool you. You're all in this book. You helped me write it by being you. You're important. You're powerful. And you're enough. I love you. Thank you for allowing me to be a part of your journey, and thank you for being a part of mine.

I want to give a special thanks to my writing mentor, my beta readers, my editor, and my artist. I met Rita Herron when I was born. She was my mom's best friend, and she helped my mom survive through one of the toughest times in her life. She's a successful writer with many award-winning titles, but she selflessly took time this past year to mentor me through my first novel, and thank-you will never be enough. I would not have a *good* book without the insight and edits from Emily Jennings, Ford Jones IV, Trena Berry, Angie McLane, Cortney Hodges, and Scott Ludwig. They all helped me take a hard look at myself as a writer and helped me develop characters as contributors instead of just sidebars. Readers have them to thank for my idea becoming a story. Thank you for mustering through all the misspelled Michaels and double exclamation points of the first draft. To Jessica Palmer, we seem to keep crossing paths to do good for the world, and I'm here for it. You are a badass with a phenomenal brain, and your editing and encouragement have helped me tremendously. And Sydney, you know my soul, and the art you created for this novel proves it. Thank you for creating my vision. You all are a part of the production of this book, and I'm grateful beyond words.

Now the hardest part: to my children. Graham, you're my heart. Everything I did to get better was because of you. Your ability to feel and connect are constant reminders that I want to live my life in the present and experience the beauty that the world has to offer. I hope you know that I'll do anything I can to make you feel safe and loved, and you are the boy I always knew I needed in my life. God makes no mistakes. Keep fighting to understand yourself and how you want to view the world to maximize your quality of life. The world is better because you're in it. I love you G. Anna Blue, you're my soul. I went to treatment so I could be the role model I wish I'd had as a young woman growing up, and my hard work has paid off. Your confidence is infectious, and I'm reminded daily that it's possible to truly love yourself completely. I know we will be best friends one day, and honestly, it makes me giddy to think about. I'm blessed to watch you glide through life with a song and a smile, and I'll always be there to catch you when you fall, which is a lot. You get it from your mama. I love you, Blue.

Best for last, to my Fuder, you deserve an award. When others would have run for the hills, you took my hand and helped me climb. You've been called to love a woman who's a storm, and you appreciate my unique view of the world and allow me to exist in the most beautiful way. Thank you for that. This book is about us. It's about our journey, and I'm grateful that we continue to fight for our happiness as a family while also pursuing our own happiness within ourselves. We've just gotten to the good part in our story, and I can't wait to see what happens next. I know it will involve moving water, green moss, rocky climbs, and serene sunsets. Thank you for doing this life with me—you and I...and the cats.

Lastly, to myself, you did it. *Bravo*. Now go live the life of freedom and love that you've cultivated. You've earned it.

Music appreciation

I would like to thank the following artists and song-writers for this badass playlist that I listened to on repeat while writing this book. Your music has gotten me through life thus far, and its significance in the time it was experienced helped me get back to the place and time I was when I needed your message to stay afloat. The music gave me an escape while the lyrics made me feel as if someone in the world understood me even when I didn't understand myself. In my mind, you're my friends, and I pray that you feel the love and appreciation of all of us for sharing your gift with the world. This is not the poetic thank-you that you deserve, but I hope you take this book as my gratitude. You helped me keep the wolves at bay.

Love,
Brooke

Ruby Blue's playlist

1. "Million Reasons," Lady Gaga
2. "I'm on Fire," Bruce Springsteen
3. "Paradise," Coldplay
4. "Grey Street," Dave Matthews Band
5. "July," Noah Cyrus
6. "Jane Says," Jane's Addiction
7. "Better Man," Taylor's Version
8. "Wagon Wheel," Old Crow Medicine Show
9. "Wonderwall," Oasis
10. "Champagne High," Sister Hazel
11. "Annalee," Yonder Mountain String Band
12. "High," Miley Cyrus
13. "I Won't Back Down," Tom Petty
14. "Black," Dierks Bentley
15. "Skinny Love," Bon Iver
16. "Rivers and Roads," The Head and the Heart
17. "Counting Stars," OneRepublic
18. "Unsteady," X Ambassadors
19. "Sign of the Times," Harry Styles
20. "Glorious," Macklemore
21. "Starting Over," Chris Stapleton
22. "You and Me," Dave Matthews Band

ABOUT THE AUTHOR

Brooke Heberling is a force to be reckoned with. She is a fierce Leo with a big heart, and she loves God, the universe, her family, her cats, her students, music that hits her soul, and beautiful crystals. Her dream has always been to be a writer who uses her strength and struggles to help others not feel so alone. She has been a freshman English teacher since graduating from Mississippi State University in 2007. She's fought hard to live her best life, and her dream is to sit by the mountain stream and create stories of hope for years to come.

Connect with her on all her social media accounts:

- Instagram: @authorbrookeheberling
- Facebook: Brooke Heberling
- TikTok: @brooke_heberling